Learning Through Supervised Practice in Student Affairs

For future student affairs professionals and higher education administrators, the supervised practice experience is where theory learned in the classroom is put into practice. *Learning Through Supervised Practice in Student Affairs* assists students in applying leadership, advising, conflict management, and planning skills to their practice. This important book explores the theories that foster learning and understanding of higher education organizations, while exercises, reflection activities, and case studies illuminate the skill areas that students must develop to become successful practitioners.

This second edition includes:

- Reflection activities to engage students and foster critical thinking
- Expanded attention to diverse populations and cultural differences
- Updated legal references and case law related to daily practice
- Broadened discussion of professional standards and alignment with the CAS standards and ACPA/NASPA's joint statement on professional competencies
- A new chapter addressing campus politics and organizational culture.

Learning Through Supervised Practice in Student Affairs bridges the gap between theory and practice, assisting students and site supervisors in constructing a practicum or internship experience that successfully contributes to learning and professional development.

Steven M. Janosik is associate professor of educational leadership and policy studies, program coordinator for the Higher Education Program, and chair of the Department of Educational Leadership at Virginia Tech.

Diane L. Cooper is professor of college student affairs administration at the University of Georgia.

Sue A. Saunders is extension professor and coordinator of the Higher Education and Student Affairs Administration Program at the University of Connecticut.

Joan B. Hirt is professor of higher education at Virginia Tech.

Learning Through Supervised Practice in Student Affairs

Second Edition

Steven M. Janosik, Diane L. Cooper,
Sue A. Saunders, and Joan B. Hirt

Routledge
Taylor & Francis Group

NEW YORK AND LONDON

Second edition published 2015
by Routledge
711 Third Avenue, New York, NY 10017

and by Routledge
2 Park Square, Milton Park, Abingdon, Oxon, OX14 4RN

Routledge is an imprint of the Taylor & Francis Group, an informa business

© 2015 Taylor & Francis

The right of Steven M. Janosik, Diane L. Cooper, Sue A. Saunders, and Joan B. Hirt to be identified as authors of this work has been asserted by them in accordance with sections 77 and 78 of the Copyright, Designs and Patents Act 1988.

First edition published by Routledge 2002

Library of Congress Cataloging-in-Publication Data
Janosik, Steven M. (Steven Michael)
  Learning through supervised practice in student affairs / Steven M. Janosik, Diane L. Cooper, and Sue A. Saunders. — Second edition.
    pages cm
  Includes bibliographical references and index.
  1. Student affairs services—Administration. 2. Student affairs administrators—Training of. 3. Student counselors—Training of.
I. Cooper, Diane L. II. Saunders, Sue A. (Sue Ann), 1950–
  LB2342.9.L43 2014
  378.1′01—dc23
  2013050443

ISBN: 978-0-415-53433-8 (hbk)
ISBN: 978-0-415-53434-5 (pbk)
ISBN: 978-0-203-11346-2 (ebk)

Typeset in Minion
by Apex CoVantage, LLC

Contents

Preface

"Learning by doing" has been an important part of most professional preparation programs (Dewey, 1916), including higher education and student affairs. In fact, many graduate students comment that their field experiences are some of the most powerful learning experiences in their programs of study (Sherman & Crum, 2009). During these experiences, students gain knowledge about the profession, acquire skills and experiences, and learn about the values and dispositions crucial to becoming successful practitioners.

Not surprisingly, these organized experiences are known by a variety of names in different programs. Practicum, internship, externship, field placement, field study, fieldwork, and field observation are just a few of the terms used to describe supervised experiences in our preparation programs. In many programs, the term *practicum* is used to designate supervised practice in master's programs and the term *internship* is used in doctoral programs. In other programs, faculty members and students use the terms interchangeably. For purposes of this book, we use the term internship as a single designator for all supervised practice regardless of the student's academic status.

This text has been developed for use by graduate students, preparation program faculty, and functional area site supervisors in higher education and student affairs. We believe that this resource serves as the only nationally available comprehensive resource that addresses this out-of-class learning experience. Our hope is that the contents of this second edition will provide a guide and a structure where the relevant theory, knowledge, reflection, the application of skills, institutional resources, and organizational politics of this experience can be examined. Astute students can learn much about themselves as persons, as future higher education administrators, and as participants in the social, educational, and political institution known as higher education.

The principles and applications presented in this book are pertinent to a variety of areas of higher education administration and a wide range of institutional types. However, examples of ethical standards and historical references have been restricted to the field of student affairs because it is the only administrative specialty with well-defined and explicitly stated values and canons of professional practice (Miller, 2001). This book is not intended for use in internships or practica where the primary purpose is to train licensed counselors,

social workers, or other mental health professionals. The focus of field placements in these specialties is to train professionals who plan to work in therapeutic relationships with individuals. Administrative internships, the subject of
this book, focus on areas such as outcomes assessment, program development,
program execution, evaluation, and organizational management and administration.

What's New in This Edition?

The first edition of this book was published in 2002. Since that time, we have
reflected on our work and received feedback from many of our faculty colleagues and students in preparation programs from across the country. Staff
members at Routledge have also helped shape this revised volume. Some of the
changes are highlighted here:

Significant new material has been added to this edition. To help students
identify their goals and learning outcomes connected with their internships, we
have added a discussion of ACPA and NASPA's joint statement on professional
competencies (ACPA/NASPA, 2010) along with the Basic Skills Self-Assessment
as new resources. These materials can be found in Chapter 2 and Appendix 2.

In this revision of the book, we have eliminated the standalone chapter on
theory. Our thinking was that a discussion of psychosocial and cognitive theories would have been more thoroughly addressed in introductory courses that
would have been taken earlier in a student's plan of study and that other theoretical issues would be better positioned in their respective chapters.

We have also updated legal references and the case law used to explain the
important legal considerations connected with daily practice and the internship
experience. We have broadened the discussion on professional standards and
ethics by including the CAS Statement of Shared Ethical Principles and introduced the importance of recognizing cultural differences when confronted with
the challenge of ethical dilemmas. These new additions are found in Chapter 5.

Finally, we have introduced a new standalone chapter that addresses campus
politics and organizational culture. Students and faculty members who used
the first edition of this book requested that more attention be given to these two
topics, and we think Chapter 6 will serve as a welcome resource.

Organization of the Book

The book is organized into three parts, and each part includes two chapters. Part
One of the book is devoted to the philosophies and theories connected to reflective learning and the structure of supervised practice. Here, we lay the foundation for a sound structured-learning experience. In Part Two we emphasize the
interpersonal dynamics between individuals—the student and the supervisor.
In particular, we address the supervision and evaluation processes. This interaction is the key to reflective learning and intentional development. In Part Three
we focus on the organization by emphasizing the legal and ethical issues related

to supervised practice in the work setting and by addressing organizational dynamics, which includes institutional culture and politics. By attending systematically to each of these domains, the student and the supervisor can ensure they are fully prepared to create a rich and rewarding internship that will meet the educational and professional needs of both parties.

Each chapter contains instructive material based on established theory, research, the authors' experiences as administrators and teachers, and the established best practices in the field. Case studies appear in several chapters; they present a variety of scenarios that students may encounter in their internships. Our hope is that students will explore the issues presented and contemplate how they might respond.

Interspersed within these materials are questions and exercises that are intended to help students reflect on their experiences, their learning, and their development. Students should complete these exercises and share their responses with their site supervisors, faculty supervisors, or peers. Discussions that ensue will enhance the learning that occurs from the experience.

A short description of each chapter appears in the paragraphs that follow.

Chapter 1: Foundations and Philosophy of Supervised Practice

In this chapter, we provide an overview of the supervised practice experience. We present a description of an intentional student affairs practitioner, the components of which constitute the learning domains essential for professional practice. Depending on the precise nature of the supervised practice, effective experiences should address all of these learning domains and competencies to varying degrees. These learning domains can be seen as targets: potential goals to contemplate as one begins a new supervised practice experience. The chapter also incorporates adult and experiential learning theories that can help students and supervisors conceptualize and plan their approaches for supervised learning experiences. Finally, we discuss specific ways that students can enter a new supervised practice site so that learning from the particular office will be most powerful.

Chapter 2: Structure and Design of the Internship

Designing an appropriate internship experience that benefits the student, the site supervisor, and the office in which the internship is located takes some time and forethought. In this chapter, we define a model that includes six components that will help both parties reach this goal. They include (a) conducting a personal skills assessment, (b) setting realistic expectations, (c) developing a contract for the experience, (d) understanding the roles and the pedagogy of the experience, (e) identifying the resources necessary to conduct the experience, and (f) balancing the experience with other curriculum components and student lives. Each of these elements should be negotiated in good faith by the site supervisor and the student, acknowledging that there may have to be some compromise. Students may have to realize that they will not be offered every opportunity they seek and that, on occasion, they may have to perform tasks that may not contribute much to their learning objectives. On the other hand, site supervisors may have to remember that interns are not full-time employees and that the interns' primary responsibility is to their education.

We believe that by using this model, students and site supervisors will be able to address expectations, roles, resources, and balance in a constructive manner that, in the end, produces a satisfying experience for all concerned.

Chapter 3: Supervision and Other Relationships That Support Learning

In this chapter, we explain the nature of the supervision relationship as well as strategies an intern can use to gain the most benefit from all of the relationships available in a supervised practice site. Further, we discuss ways to avoid or cope with common problems that may occur. More specifically, we review the context of supervision, variability of sites, the development of the supervisory relationship, the supervisor's roles and functions, and expectations for students. Finally, we provide a variety of tips on how interns can improve their potential for success.

Chapter 4: The Evaluation Process

This chapter explores the evaluative process as an ongoing set of activities that will help students maximize learning in the supervised practice experience. We discuss both formative and summative evaluation processes and the interactive activities necessary to maximize the interrelationships between the experience, theories, personal knowledge, and individual professional values. We also highlight the importance of reflection as a learning pedagogy.

Students need to take an active role in the evaluation of the internship site, the supervision received, and their own performance. Learning to give and receive constructive feedback is an important skill that students should develop as early as possible. Tips on how to close the internship experience are also discussed.

Chapter 5: Legal and Ethical Issues

There is no escaping the fact that the higher education enterprise is a highly regulated environment. Daily practice is complicated by a myriad of legal mandates, rules, and regulations. The purpose of this chapter is to highlight a number of important legal and ethical issues that should be addressed early in any supervised experience. By doing so, interns will have a clear understanding of the parameters of acceptable behavior and will be less likely to accidentally breach laws and rules that govern professional practice and will not inadvertently stumble into illegal or unethical behavior. Topics reviewed in this chapter include formal and informal working relationships, questions of authority and responsibility, liability issues, liability management, compensation issues, and professional ethics and standards.

Chapter 6: Understanding Organizational Contexts

The last chapter of this book addresses the nature of organizations and defines several mechanisms through which organizations can be viewed and understood. We describe three of the most common organizational theories (also known as *lenses*) individuals use to describe how organizations operate. These are known as the structural lens, the human resource lens, and the biological lens. Two additional perspectives that are particularly useful for student affairs professionals are also described: the political and the cultural. Each perspective is introduced, and its usefulness and its limitations are discussed.

Through a variety of exercises, we encourage students to identify their dominant lens, expand their repertoire of perspectives, and develop tools to address organizational issues from multiple perspectives as a way to create a better understanding of the organizations in which they work. By doing so, we believe that interns and professionals will be better situated to generate multiple responses to workplace issues and to succeed in a variety of professional capacities.

Acknowledgments

First, we want to acknowledge the contributions Don Creamer and Roger Winston made on the first edition of this work. Both played crucial roles in the conceptualization and development of that book. While both are enjoying retirement and have become less active as researchers and writers in recent years, their influence on this edition is still significant. They continue to have a profound effect on their colleagues, students, and the profession, and for that we are extremely grateful. We are honored to call them colleagues and friends.

Second, we want to honor the collaborative nature of this project. Each chapter was written by a lead author and reviewed by a second member of the writing team. Each chapter was read and reviewed twice by other members of the writing team. We have done our best to integrate what we have written and reduce as much duplication as we can, while acknowledging that repetition can sometimes be a good teacher.

Finally, we would like to thank our many students who have taught us much more about supervised practice than they realized. We also wish to acknowledge the many higher education administrators who as site supervisors graciously shared their time with our students and their constructive feedback with us. In particular, we would like to thank two colleagues, David Clokey, from the University of Connecticut, and Tiffany J. Davis, from North Carolina State University, who have directly influenced our perspectives on how to best make internships powerful learning opportunities.

Steven M. Janosik

Diane L. Cooper

Sue A. Saunders

Joan B. Hirt

References

American College Personnel Association (ACPA)/National Association of Student Affairs Administrators (NASPA). (2010). *Professional competency areas for student affairs practitioners.* Washington, DC: American College Personnel Association and National Association of Student Personnel Administrators.

Dewey, J. (1916). *Democracy in education: An introduction to the philosophy of education.* New York, NY: Macmillan.

Miller, T. K. (Ed.) (2001). *The CAS book of professional standards for higher education.* Washington, DC: Council for the Advancement of Standards in Higher Education.

Sherman, W. H., & Crum, K. S. (2009). Designing the internship in educational leadership as a transformative tool for improved practice. *International Journal of Educational Reform, 18*(1), 63–81.

Part One

1   Foundations and Philosophy of Supervised Practice

In the earliest days of student affairs work, the Student Personnel Point of View (American Council on Education, 1937) emphasized educating "the whole person" so that individuals can reach their full potential as the essential purpose of the student affairs profession (Roberts, 2012). The higher education landscape has changed dramatically in the 75 years that have followed. Students are increasingly diverse in terms of age, ethnicity, socioeconomic status, sexual orientation, gender identities, career goals, personal philosophies, political preferences, and reliance on technologies unimagined among students of previous generations. New roles have emerged for administrators in higher education, such as work with graduate students, engagement with alumni in mutually beneficial ways, and providing risk management guidance. Higher education institutions have also changed. We see new approaches not envisioned just a few years ago happening with increasing speed, such as massive online learning initiatives, new academic majors related to technology, appealing building amenities, branding strategies to attract donors, and substantial efforts to contribute to the economic development of communities and states.

The pace and complexity of change among students and institutions will likely increase (Levine & Dean, 2012; Selingo, 2013). Therefore, student affairs professionals will be required to manage contexts that are continually more ambiguous and where students and other constituents desire a much greater degree of responsiveness. How then does a new student affairs professional balance commitment to the core purpose of enabling students to reach their full potential (Lampkin, 2007) with the challenges of working within increasingly complex higher education institutions?

It becomes ever more important that practitioners learn quickly and continuously; they must know their values, skills, and how they learn best. Effective preparation for the student affairs profession includes both classroom instruction and supervised practical experience, such as internships or graduate assistantships (Council for the Advancement of Standards in Higher Education [CAS], 2012). Formal classroom education alone—with specified learning outcomes, regular and structured feedback, and educational experiences carefully designed by the instructor—is necessary, but not sufficient, to prepare students for the daily struggle of professional practice. Although supervised practice experiences have historically been required components of preparation pro-grams' curricula (McEwen & Talbot, 1977), carefully designed and executed experiences are even more critical learning opportunities for enabling new pro-fessionals to thrive within the rapidly changing higher education milieu.

Through a practicum, assistantship, or internship experience, students learn nimble thinking, recognize the nuances in a workplace, read the intentions of coworkers and supervisors, and take individual initiative to create solutions that fit the organizational culture. With the guidance of a faculty or site supervisor, students are able to address real-world issues and develop tacit knowledge— the kind of practical wisdom that allows for seemingly intuitive problem solv-ing (Reber, 1993). In addition, supervised experience develops a trajectory of increasingly complex thinking that will likely generalize to new situations, such as those encountered in a first professional position (Sheckley & Keeton, 2001).

The structure of the supervised experience as well as the skill of both the fac-ulty and site supervisors are key variables in determining whether a particular internship will meet the lofty goals of developing practical wisdom and com-plex problem solving. However, an equally important determinant of the value of a supervised practical experience is the individual student's ability to know and adapt his or her learning approaches, even if it means using a style that is not comfortable or natural.

Reflection Activity

Take a look at the following two stories—one of Marcia and one of Elliott. Each story describes very different desires for the supervised practice expe-rience. As you read the stories, think of which elements of each person's approach are most like your preferences and which are least like your prefer-ences. Then, reflect on the questions that follow each story.

Marcia—Marcia has a reputation within her cohort as the one who can best go with the flow. She is very creative, often identifying novel, unexpected solutions to the problems that are presented. Sometimes her solutions are unrealistic or the implementation is less attentive to details. However, her intuitive understanding of students' needs often makes her ideas very pow-erful contributions, especially to the case study and simulation exercises required in her student development and leadership courses.

Marcia wants to find an internship site that will allow her to be creative and where she can work independently. She wants a supervisor who will let her explore possibilities rather than providing too much structure. She wants an open-minded supervisor who is willing to help her make sense of her observations. She does not want a site that requires substantial assessment or writing tasks since she would prefer working directly with students because their needs are often unpredictable.

Marcia wants her schedule to be flexible so that she can take advantage of the unexpected things that she might learn through observation and problem solving. She is open to a wide variety of experiences, even those that are planned at the last minute.

Elliott—His fellow students and faculty members know El as an excellent planner. He has an extraordinary capacity to manage details and to make sure that every possible contingency is covered. Although he is reliable and consistent in his classwork performance, there are times when he has trouble finding creative solutions to problems in the moment.

When thinking about a supervised practice experience, Elliott indicates he wants a supervisor who gives clear direction and detailed guidance—especially before Elliott makes a decision. Elliott's goal is to make sure that he does his tasks correctly, so he hopes that early in the experience the supervisor will share details about the history and context of the site so that he can design workable plans.

Elliott would prefer writing, assessment, and project-planning tasks to be the central focus of the supervised practice experience. With these types of tasks, he could better control achievement of his specific goals and outcomes for the experience. It is important for Elliott to have a predictable schedule, since he knows he is more effective when he can anticipate what tasks can be expected and planned for.

Assumption: In nearly all student affairs offices, elements of both Marcia's and Elliott's approaches would be useful, depending on the specific situation. The following questions will help you articulate your natural preferences and others that may not be preferred but need to be developed.

Questions

1. Which of the two stories is most like you (even if it is not exactly a match) in terms of these elements:
    a. Preferred relationship with supervisor?
    b. Preferred degree of personal control of the activities?
    c. Preferred degree of structure provided by the site?
    d. Preferred degree of prior planning?
    e. Other elements?
2. Describe in detail your preferences in terms of these elements:
    a. Preferred relationship with supervisor?
    b. Preferred degree of personal control of the activities?
    c. Preferred degree of structure provided by the site?
    d. Preferred degree of prior planning?
    e. Other elements?

3. Describe what would be least preferable in terms of these elements:
    a. Preferred relationship with supervisor?
    b. Preferred degree of personal control of the activities?
    c. Preferred degree of structure provided by the site?
    d. Preferred degree of prior planning?
    e. Other elements?
4. How might you develop your capacity as a learner in your upcoming supervised practice experience? Think about how you can stretch beyond your natural preferences.

Purpose of Chapter 1

In this chapter, we provide an overview of the supervised practice experience. We present a description of an intentional student affairs practitioner, the components of which constitute the learning domains essential for professional practice. Depending on the precise nature of the supervised practice, effective experiences should address all of these learning domains and competencies, to varying degrees. These learning domains can be seen as targets—potential goals to contemplate as one begins a new supervised practice experience. The chapter also incorporates adult and experiential learning theories that can help students and supervisors conceptualize and plan their approaches for supervised learning experiences. Finally, we discuss specific ways that students can enter a new supervised practice site so that learning from the particular office will be most powerful.

What Is Supervised Practice?

Since the middle of the last century, scholars have contended that a structured application of practice component is essential for graduate preparation in student affairs (Delworth & Hanson, 1980; Greenleaf, 1977; Knock, 1977; McGlothlin, 1964). Currently, the most recent CAS requirements for master's-level student affairs preparation programs mandate that a structured practical experience be included as part of a graduate preparation program. Specifically, these standards mandate that students complete "[a] minimum of 300 hours of supervised practice, consisting of at least two distinct experiences" (CAS, 2012, p. 356).

Although student affairs professionals at all levels can benefit from material in this book, students enrolled in a preparation program at the master's or doctoral level and who desire a career in higher education administration are the primary audience. For the purposes of this book, several conditions are necessary for an experience to be categorized as supervised practice. First, the supervised practice experience is designed to give students an opportunity to engage in meaningful professional-level work. Some examples of meaningful professional-level work include advising individual students, planning alumni programs, managing student organization budgets, facilitating workshops, or supervising paraprofessionals. During supervised practice, the student's experience occurs as part of the work of an office or functional unit in a higher education institution. Part of the power of supervised practice is the connection between the student's intentions and the constraints or opportunities imposed by a particular organizational environment—with its distinctive culture, politics, power structure, and leadership. Finally, a more seasoned administrator in a college or university carefully supervises the experience.

Many types of experiences can be classified as supervised practice in this context, including these:

1. Graduate assistantships. In these roles, students are paid paraprofessionals charged to accomplish regular and sustained job duties. Most often, students are evaluated on the degree to which they contribute to the initiatives of the office that employs them. Students' achievement of their own learning objectives is most often not the primary emphasis of the experience.
2. Volunteer supervised experiences. In many preparation programs, master's or doctoral students are recruited to provide short-term programs or services that are unpaid or for which they are given a small honorarium. These might include facilitating workshops or trainings, teaching a discussion section of a course, or advising a student organization. In these experiences, students do not receive academic credit.
3. Internships that are not for credit. Master's or doctoral students may take on a fixed-duration supervised internship where there is no credit offered, but students receive remuneration for expenses or a stipend, or both. For instance, several professional organizations (e.g., National Orientation Directors Association [NODA]; Association of College and University Housing Officers-International [ACUHO-I]) offer these types of opportunities during the summer. Within some preparation programs students can earn academic credit for classes associated with these professional association–sponsored internships or for other summer internships.
4. Internships that receive credit. Master's or doctoral students take on supervised practice experiences that last for a fixed duration and that are often unpaid. On many campuses these experiences are termed *practicums*. Their primary purpose is to further students' learning goals, although internship students also provide assistance to the sponsoring office in service-delivery, program-planning, or other tasks. Supervision in this type of internship typically involves two individuals: the site supervisor, who is a staff member in the office sponsoring the internship, and the academic supervisor, who is a faculty member. (Chapter 3 contains more details how to work with supervisors in a variety of institutional roles.)

Although the material contained in this book can easily be adapted for all of the supervised practice experiences outlined previously, there is particular emphasis on experiences that occur in conjunction with an academic course.

The Intentional Student Affairs Practitioner

Student affairs practitioners are expected to fulfill a variety of roles within their institutions; paramount among them are educator, leader, and manager (Creamer, Winston, & Miller, 2001). These roles carry with them certain values and a need for theoretical knowledge, ethical strictures, applied knowledge, and skills that enable professionals to facilitate both the formal and informal processes of learning in colleges and universities. They are humanists and pragmatists (Winston & Saunders, 1991) who enable the achievement of potential in the people with whom they work, yet they are managers of resources and of people who must achieve institutional as well as individual aims. All of these roles must be conducted in an ethical environment where all educational activities are firmly and directly targeted to achieve the most basic purposes of education: individual and community development.

Figure 1.1 depicts the seven learning domains that should be addressed and revisited by student affairs professionals as they journey through their careers.

Figure 1.1 Model of professional identity.

Although most professional preparation programs include these domains in their curriculum, the achievement of these comprehensive educational objectives is certainly not fully realized at the close of a master's or doctoral program. The domains are related to the more specific professional competencies developed by the American College Personnel Association/National Association of Student Affairs Professionals (ACPA/NASPA) (2010) and also to a number of research articles that identify the salient professional competencies required of new professionals (Cuyjet, Longwell-Grice, & Molina, 2009; Herdlein, 2004; Lovell & Kosten, 2000; Renn & Hodges, 2007; Waple, 2006) and more advanced doctoral graduates (Saunders & Cooper, 1999). Attending to these learning domains is integral to achieving the educational goals of supervised practice.

Addressing the learning domains, however, is not enough to realize the maximum benefit from a supervised practice experience. These learning domains are inextricably entwined with one's professional identity that encompasses beliefs about professional behavior, management philosophy, and effective learning strategies among other elements. Fundamentally, professional identity is the way professionals define themselves, as well as their integrity in translating that definition to practice. Professional identity is the lens that interprets the meaning of the seven learning domains and fosters their application to authentic professional practice.

In no particular hierarchy, the learning domains are scholarly knowledge, applied knowledge, professional ethics, technical skills, interpersonal skills, inclusive practice skills, and organizational leadership skills.

Scholarly Knowledge

One of the defining characteristics of a profession is the existence of a body of scholarship that informs and provides a framework for what practitioners do. Two fundamental categories of scholarly knowledge are theory and research. The intentional student affairs practitioner is conversant in both. Further, intentional student affairs practitioners keep up with the newest developments in theories and research.

Knowing formal theories relevant to students, organizations, and research is an endeavor essential for effective practice. According to Jones and Abes (2011), theory has six purposes: describe, explain, predict, influence outcomes, assess practice, and generate new knowledge and research. There are a number of different kinds of theories, such as student learning and development; organizational, management, and leadership; individual and group intervention; and assessment, evaluation, and research that the CAS (2012) include as requirements for professional preparation programs.

Staying current with empirical research provides an invaluable resource to guide practice. Both qualitative and quantitative research from student affairs and related fields provide carefully analyzed descriptions of students' characteristics and best practices to promote students' learning and organizational effectiveness.

Attending to scholarly knowledge through reading and discussion of theory and research is often seen as an activity of lesser importance in supervised practice. However, it is important that both the student and supervisors focus on enhancing relevant scholarly knowledge as an outcome of the experience. For example, if a student is working with an unfamiliar functional area or student population, one early learning activity should be reading, discussing, or writing about theories and research studies that will provide important context for the subsequent practical experience.

Applied Knowledge

Applied knowledge develops through experimentation and repetition. It comes about through trying (often repeatedly) to identify the ways in which the principles derived from theories and research exhibit themselves in the complexity of real-world practice. Further, it involves the attempts to try out these principles and then to analyze what worked and what did not. For instance, one can study the physical dynamics involved in riding a bicycle, but the first time one attempts to mount and ride a bicycle, the experience is somewhat frightening when the rider discovers the difficulty of simultaneously maintaining balance, steering, and pedaling. With practice under a variety of conditions and terrain, individuals acquire an applied knowledge that enables them to navigate difficult circumstances with little conscious thought about the physical dynamics of riding a bicycle. Through practice and careful attention to detail, bike riding eventually becomes second nature.

Applied knowledge in student affairs is acquired through a variety of ways, such as through extensive contact with students and other constituencies or by designing programs and policies that effect positive change in students or institutions. In essence, professionals use these experiences to create informal theory, which often guides practice (Love, 2012). However, Evans and Guido (2012) state that this informal theory is not sufficient to serve as a basis for practice, since "it is impossible to determine the accuracy of assumptions or sense making" (p. 199). Therefore, this applied knowledge must be combined with an understanding of the scholarly knowledge of research and theories as described earlier.

Supervised practice experiences are especially useful ways to develop applied knowledge since students observe how the hypotheses of scholarly knowledge work (or do not work) in real-world contexts. With use of the appropriate learning strategies described later in this book, these observations can evolve into meaningful theories in use.

Professional Ethics

Student affairs practitioners are faced daily with situations that involve conflicting personal interests, values, belief systems, and goals. Practitioners must determine what is right or what ought to be done within legal and institutional policy parameters. "Ethical beliefs and belief systems are intended to serve as guides to action in confusing and difficult circumstances" (Fried, 1997, p. 5). Professional ethical standards and principles are potential guides for student affairs professionals in ambiguous circumstances where there is no clear right course of action or where there may be multiple right choices (Nash, 1997). However, ethical standards do not constitute a simplistic recipe for behaving professionally. In a few instances ethical standards statements will give explicit rules about behavior or actions to avoid, but in most situations student affairs professionals must make nuanced judgments about the meaning of the ethical principles and other contextual factors that undergird the standards.

Ethical principles such as do no harm, promote justice, respect autonomy, or benefit others (American College Personnel Association, 2006) may provide flexible criteria to rely on when making complex decisions. But because these general principles contain positivist assumptions that there is an objective or universally agreed-upon ethical course of action, they should be applied carefully (Fried, 2011). With the increasing globalization of higher education along with the need to recognize both dominant and nondominant voices (Fried, 2011), promoting dialogue and deep reflection about the nature of a particular dilemma, one's values and beliefs, and the perhaps conflicting perspectives of others are necessary steps to take when trying to develop a pattern of ethical practice (Magolda & Baxter Magolda, 2011). Because of the overriding concern regarding ways one can engage in ethical practice, ethical issues are discussed more fully in Chapter 5.

The internship experience allows students the opportunity to observe situations that have ethical implications and to see how practitioners address—or perhaps fail to address—them. During the internship experience students may also find themselves involved in activities in which they must analyze and determine the appropriate course of ethical action.

Technical Skills

Student affairs practitioners are expected to possess a wide array of specialized skills, some of which are acquired directly through professional preparation and others that are acquired prior to beginning a professional preparation program. Examples of some technical skills today's student affairs professionals are expected to possess include technology skills (such as creating webpages; using social media, such as Facebook or Twitter; using various types of computer software; managing databases), program planning, data analysis, program evaluation strategies, determining learning outcomes, or selecting appropriate pedagogy. Other skills may be acquired through formal or informal means and include, for instance, how to run a meeting, recruit student participants, create flyers, devise publicity campaigns, and negotiate contracts for vendors. Many of the latter skills may have been acquired while functioning as a student or community leader.

Through observing practitioners and assuming responsibility for tasks, projects, and activities associated with the ongoing operation of the site, students have multiple opportunities to acquire technical and practical skills needed to become a competent student affairs professional.

Interpersonal Skills

Most successful student affairs professionals possess good people skills; that is, they are able to communicate effectively and build harmonious, amicable, cooperative relationships with students and colleagues. They also possess basic personality characteristics that attract them to working with others and have a desire to be of service. Although these interpersonal characteristics and intentions to be helpful are an important foundation, effective use of interpersonal skills with individuals and groups requires both formal training and supervised practice. Students and, in many cases, colleagues require high-quality guidance, support, and critique that entails greater skill than simply good intentions.

Specifically, the Professional Competency Areas for Student Affairs Practitioners (ACPA/NASPA, 2010) outline a number of basic interpersonal skills useful for advising and helping students and colleagues. Among these are developing active listening competence, facilitating problem solving, encouraging effective decision making, and managing conflicts. Through formal training and supervised practice, students can sharpen their interpersonal skills and build effective advising and helping skills.

Effective interpersonal skills are far more comprehensive conceptually than simply listening, helping, and advising. Developing workable relationships with students and colleagues also requires establishing a professional and confident demeanor, knowing when and with whom to share information, constructing written or oral communications with a tone appropriate for the task, and ensuring that one transmits information in an accurate and accessible way. Often called *soft skills,* these competencies are best learned by observing role models, reflecting on one's attempts to use excellent interpersonal skills, and perhaps most importantly, receiving positive and critical feedback from others. In everyday life, critiquing another's interpersonal skills is not a common practice; thus, internship students and supervisors should commit to giving and receiving forthright feedback about areas of practice that can be emotionally sensitive, such as demeanor and confidence.

Inclusive Practice Skills

During the past 20 years, student affairs professionals have carefully examined multicultural competence—defining knowledge, skills, and awareness components that are needed to create campus environments that are equitable for all, including students and constituents from all social identity groups and from both dominant and subordinate groups on any particular campus (Pope, Reynolds, & Mueller, 2004). Inclusive practice skills involve personal awareness of one's social identity and its effect on one's professional identity. This personal awareness needs to be coupled with recognition of how such concepts as stereotype threat, privilege, and oppression manifest in the student and organizational cultures. Personal awareness and conceptual knowledge are foundations for the actual ability to work with students and other constituents in inclusive and equitable ways. Specifically, student affairs professionals need to possess the ability to facilitate dialogues among people from disparate groups and to effectively engage with diverse individuals in ways that reflect an appreciation of cultural and human differences (ACPA/ NASPA, 2010).

Even though there have been many efforts to infuse perspectives of diverse groups into the theoretical and research fabric of student affairs work, there is limited evidence that this scholarly work has been consistently translated into higher education administrative practice (Pope, Reynolds, & Mueller, 2004). The current higher education landscape is characterized by increased diversity, so it is even more important than in previous generations that intentional student affairs practitioners hone their inclusive practice skills. Supervised practice experiences often provide many ways to think about and expand those skills.

Supervised practice experiences can provide valuable opportunities for students to address the Equity, Diversity, and Inclusion Competencies identified in the ACPA and NASPA (2010) identification of professional competency areas. Specifically, internship students can observe the ways in which experienced professionals design programs that address the needs of diverse students and promote respectful dialogue. In addition, supervised practice experiences allow students to see how professionals communicate the needs of those who may be marginalized on a particular campus. Finally, supervised practice should be structured so that an internship student can move beyond observation to participate in program and policy design and implementation that seek to promote equity and inclusion.

To most effectively build inclusive practice skills in internships, the student must be willing to think about the sometimes difficult issues around social identity difference and privilege. Further, having a supervisor willing to openly discuss the dynamics around equity or lack thereof on a particular campus is particularly helpful.

Organizational Leadership Skills

Although related to interpersonal skills, organizational leadership skills are distinguished by a fundamental ability to figure out how a particular workplace or group operates, with the attendant organizational culture context, power dynamics, evolution of roles, and development of loyalty and cohesion. Further, organizational leadership skills include a practitioner's ability to foster positive change through such strategies as building coalitions, garnering support from upper-level administrators, or inspiring colleagues to achieve more lofty outcomes.

Being a skilled organizational leader requires an ability to discern the culture of a work environment. The culture of an organization facilitates achievement of certain goals and blocks others or promotes the voices of certain leaders and thwarts others (Kuh & Whitt, 1988). It is beyond the scope of this chapter to define the often hidden but powerful manifestations of organizational cultures in student affairs and higher education workplaces. Discerning a culture is difficult, especially for those who have been embedded in an organizational culture for a long time.

Even though the task is challenging and one may never fully understand how a culture affects an organization's work, it is important for internship students to carefully analyze and reflect on their workplace culture. There are often clues found in organizational history, patterns of informal leadership, traditions, and such seemingly inconsequential patterns of behavior as lunchtime activity.

Although the duration of internships is often too brief to allow students to demonstrate all of the skills of organizational leadership, such as building coalitions or obtaining support of administrative decision makers, students can use their work with a faculty or site supervisor to think through or rehearse how a good idea might be implemented in a sustainable way. At the very least, internship students can contemplate who might be key stakeholders whose support is needed to implement an initiative or how one might frame a message to inspire students or colleagues. Further, internship students should use their time to carefully observe how the leaders in their workplace leverage their resources (either financial, time, relationship, or personnel) to ensure success of an initiative within a particular organizational environment.

Reflection Activity

Having read the section on learning domains, contemplate what you have read and answer the following questions. Then discuss your answers with your site supervisor or a faculty member.

1.   What learning domains appear most important to address in your current supervised experience? Why?

2. What learning domains are already well developed? How did you learn these skills or acquire this knowledge?
3. What learning domains do you think will be easiest to address? Why?
4. What learning domains will be most challenging to address? Why?

Professional Identity: The Link Among the Seven Learning Domains

A professional's identity answers the question "Who am I?" It encompasses what one believes about professional work along with the capacity to reevaluate and change those beliefs when confronted with dissonant information or experience. An administrator with a well-developed professional identity recognizes his or her capacity to be self-authored and to function with integrity, where both personal and professional actions are congruent with beliefs (Saunders & Lease Butts, 2011). Determining a professional identity, how it relates to one's personal life, and the location of boundaries in professional relationships are fraught with challenging questions to contemplate. For example, a professional should reasonably question whether self-disclosing personal information to a student is indeed helpful or serves to meet the professional's needs for popularity or friendship. Another common question might be, "Is reluctance to ask a supervisor for advice a function of a lack of confidence or simply of a desire to be appropriately independent?"

Professionals who want to operate at peak performance levels must understand their assumptions about who is a deserving student, what is a worthy program, and what constitutes effective management—and be willing and able to challenge those assumptions. Student affairs professionals are often privileged because of their leadership capacity, academic achievements, facility in social situations, and perhaps membership in social-identity groups that are dominant in a particular context. Recognizing those privileged statuses and challenging the ways these may negatively affect others are important elements of developing a professional identity.

Identity includes accurate assessment of strengths and deficits along with the capacity to be self-directed and self-correcting in the pursuit of self-improvement. As said by a graduate student who completed her practicum requirements, "Practicum is a time to evaluate yourself." This comment highlights the fact that good supervised practice experiences change the way students see themselves in relation to professional work. They learn that they can assume responsibility and take charge of important projects in the field. They can demonstrate professional behavior and receive feedback that helps them understand themselves as professionals. They come to feel that they possess a great deal of knowledge and skill and that they can use both in practical ways. Sometimes they also are faced with the reality of skills deficits or the realization that they are unwilling to make the personal sacrifices that certain positions require.

Fundamentally, professional identity is the glue that holds the seven other learning domains together. One's professional identity is a lens for interpreting what has been learned in these domains and what else needs to be learned. The learning that occurs through these domains also transforms one's professional identity.

Reflection Activity

Think about your professional and personal identity. Answer the following questions and discuss your answers with someone with whom you feel comfortable.

1. In what ways might your family expectations, cultural background, or prior memorable experiences influence your professional identity?
2. What are your assumptions about who are viewed as good students or what are considered to be worthy programs or effective management strategies?
3. What are potential situations that might cause difficulty in establishing appropriate boundaries?

Maximizing Learning in Supervised Experience

A substantial body of learning theory and empirical research supports the truism that "experience is the best teacher." However, simply being present in the experience will not result in the maximum depth and breadth of achievement of the learning domains outlined here or contribute fully to the evolution of a professional identity. The remainder of this chapter presents relevant adult learning theory and related processes that can guide the student and supervisors as they create meaningful learning experiences.

Kolb's Model of Experiential Learning

In the 1970s David Kolb began work on a model of experiential learning that was consistent with what was known about human cognition and understanding of the ways individuals grow and develop. The model that emerged from Kolb's research emphasized the role that experience plays in learning and outlined how experiential learning is the base for concept development, which then governs the selection of new experiences. Because the raison d'être of internships is to integrate theory, practice, and self-knowledge, an understanding of Kolb's model provides a basis for students to maximize learning in their internship experience. Kolb (1981) conceived of a four-stage cycle of learning (see Figure 1.2). To assist in understanding this model, a brief case study is presented in the next section.

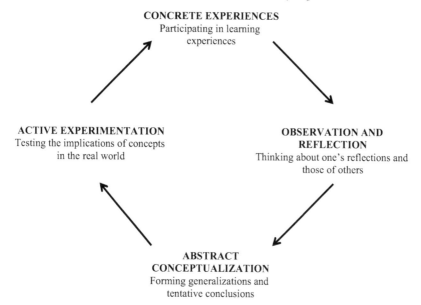

Figure 1.2 A four-stage cycle of learning.

The Case of Latisha

Concrete Experience

Suppose that Latisha is beginning her admissions office internship during her second year in a college student affairs administration program. During the first visit to the office she has many concrete experiences that can serve as the basis for observation and reflection, such as being introduced to various staff members, watching as visitors are greeted by office staff, and touring the office. As Latisha goes to meet with various admissions counselors, she finds that she is walking up and down many steps to get to the admissions counselors' offices to introduce herself to them.

Observation and Reflection

This concrete experience led Latisha to move to the observation and reflection stage of Kolb's model. Specifically, Latisha observed that a former private residence (with three floors) located adjacent to the main campus has been designated as the central admissions office where prospective students and their families meet with admissions personnel. She also noticed that the central staircase of the admissions building located just inside the front entryway contains an automatic stair-climbing device for individuals who need assistance in making their way to the offices of admissions counselors on upper floors of the building. Finally, Latisha observed that to get close to the receptionist's desk, one must descend two steps into what was formerly a 1960s-style sunken living room.

As Latisha returned to her apartment later that evening, she began to reflect on what she observed. Initially, she felt troubled about the embarrassment a mobility-disabled student might feel when asking to use the stair-climbing machine or having to talk to the receptionist from a distance of 6 or 7 feet. Her early reflections were made from the perspective of the clientele of the admissions office. She also recalled observing that almost all of the parking spaces in the lot adjacent to the building were reserved for individuals with disabilities and that there was a very attractive, accessible ramp that led to the front door. Latisha's early reflections led her to recall other observations that were consistent with Kolb's theory that links observation and reflection as integrated processes.

Also, in line with the Kolb model, Latisha tried to reflect on her observations from viewpoints other than those of the prospective students. She thought back on her conversations with and observations of staff. In her conversations with admissions counselors, she learned that the location of the admissions office was new and, when compared with the former office, was more inviting, less cramped, and easier to access by car. She also noticed that counselors and the receptionist did not stay by their desks but greeted visitors at the door. She also thought about her understanding of the admissions office mission statement: a clear statement about commitment to diversity in recruiting students from various racial, ethnic, gender-identification, and sexual-orientation groups and from populations with differing abilities. The admissions office mission statement was disseminated to prospective students in a variety of ways: on the back of business cards, in a prominent place on the website, and on a large poster located in the foyer of the building. Some salient elements of the statement were integrated into the office logo appearing on signage and stationery.

Finally, Latisha reflected on the readings from her campus environments class. These readings delved into how a culture of openness to diversity is communicated more by symbols and artifacts (such as diversity of staff, architecture of facilities, and history of the environment) than by what individuals say directly or what is written in policy statements. Latisha had observed that the staff was mostly white, young (age 22–25), and able-bodied and that the facility was decorated in a traditional fashion, rather like the lobby of an older, elite hotel or 1960s upper-middle-class home.

Abstract Conceptualization

As she spent more time reflecting on her experience, Latisha moved to the third stage of Kolb's model: forming abstract concepts and generalizations. In an attempt to integrate her observations and reflections into reasoned conclusions, Latisha believed that she could, at this stage, only draw a tentative conclusion about the degree to which the admissions office communicated an inviting atmosphere to prospective students with mobility disabilities. Even though Latisha did not have adequate information (such as enrollment and retention data about students with physical disabilities or commentary from faculty and other administrators about the environment), she felt that there was a strong possibility that the admissions office was communicating messages that would be discouraging to prospective students with disabilities.

Active Experimentation

The final stage of Kolb's model, testing implications of concepts, is particularly important for the intern. Most supervised practice experiences are relatively short in duration: one term or occasionally an entire academic year. Because of the intricacies of any campus environment, it is nearly impossible to draw conclusions that are reasoned and grounded in appropriate data in such a short time. Moreover, interns are often not privy to all the information available to full-time staff members. For example, on-site supervisors may typically try not to burden or bias student interns with information about office politics or the hidden agendas of various administrators who influence the office (especially early in the internship). Therefore, in most cases, interns who delve into the active experimentation stage are testing hypotheses rather than fully formed conclusions.

Latisha wanted to test her hypothesis about the openness of the admissions office to individuals with mobility disabilities. She wanted to raise questions but did not want to accuse the staff in the admissions office of bias, nor communicate a know-it-all attitude after having worked at the site for less than a week. So Latisha first determined the enrollment and retention data for various underrepresented populations as one way to test her hypothesis. She also decided to talk with her faculty supervisor, Tom, about how to bring this issue to the attention of her on-site supervisor in a constructive, nonthreatening way. Since the faculty supervisor knew that the on-site supervisor was open to questions from interns, he advised Latisha to simply ask how applicants with mobility disabilities manage to navigate around the admissions office and to share her questions about whether students with physical disabilities respond negatively to the facilities. As in Kolb's model, this active experimentation on Latisha's part (asking the questions of the on-site supervisor) led to concrete experience (listening to the on-site supervisor's responses) that then resulted in further observation and reflection.

The Role of Emotions, Prior Experiences, and Reflection

Newer commentary on experiential learning models, such as Kolb's, argues that rationality, with its seemingly linear and universalist perspective, is overly emphasized with the effect of marginalizing feelings and emotions (Dirkx, 2001). Yet one's emotional reactions (even though not always explainable) serve as critical component of learning and motivation. Brain-based theories of learning (Damasio, 1999; Hill, 2001; Sheckley & Bell, 2006) posit that emotions are interrelated with our ability to remember and make meaning of a particular experience. So to maximize learning in a supervised practice experience, it is important to recognize and acknowledge one's feelings rather than simply trying to discount their impact.

Other critics of more traditional theories of adult learning (Merriam, Caffarella, & Baumgartner, 2006) contended that early theories do not fully acknowledge that learning is socially constructed. Specifically, the newer learning theories posit the conclusions one draws from an experience are embedded in the context of one's social identity, such as race, ethnicity, socioeconomic status, sexual orientation, gender identity and expression, religion, and other background variables. To apply this concept to learning in the supervised practice experience, students need to think about and discuss with supervisors or mentors how their social identities and those of others in the environment frame observations, how they draw abstract conceptualizations, and what drives their choices for taking action.

Necessary conditions for application of the experiential and adult learning approaches. For interns to use experiential and adult learning theories, several conditions must be present:

- Approach actual experiences with an open mind, trying to identify and understand the potential impact of one's own preconceived notions or the conclusions of other students or colleagues.
- Observe and reflect from multiple perspectives, including perspectives drawn from one's own emotional reactions and social identity characteristics that may be relevant.
- Include more than personal conclusions in abstract conceptualization. Integrate research, theories, and seemingly disparate observations to form a reasonable hypothesis.
- Be willing to question more, take risks, and read more fully to actively and intentionally experiment when applying what one has learned.
- Recognize that experiential learning requires clear goals and ability to monitor achievement.

Opportunities to apply models of experiential learning occur repeatedly in the course of a busy intern's day. New experiences abound, and the intern is often charged with moving quickly to the active experimentation or problem-solving phase. Because the internship is indeed a learning experience, it is important that interns and their supervisors allow adequate time to work through the middle two stages of Kolb's model—observation and reflection and abstract conceptualization. Reflecting and processing one's experiences are crucial to learning.

How students can work with supervisors to enhance learning. Supervision is a critical component of maximizing learning in the internship. Although the supervision process is discussed in detail in Chapter 3, at the beginning of a new internship it is important to remember why the site or faculty supervisors' functions, or both, are so essential. Baxter Magolda and King (2004) developed a learning partnerships model designed to promote student development that contains principles with implications for internship students and their supervisors. They recommend that learners and partners (supervisors in this instance) should (a) mutually construct meaning, (b) situate learning in the experience, and (c) validate the learner's capacity to know and form conclusions. The learning partner or supervisor often initiates these principles. However, the internship student can and should take responsibility for discussing his or her observations and hypotheses. A foundation for these discussions is willingness on both sides to listen fully in an environment with few distractions and to be forthright about one's intentions and assumptions. As one begins a supervised practice experience, it is important to negotiate with the supervisors the expectations for the relationship.

Questions to guide experiential learning. In most cases, it is helpful to have a clear structure to guide discussions or reflections. The questions contained in the following Reflection Activity are designed to help students think carefully about their learning. These questions can be used in supervisory conversations and the evaluation process (discussed in Chapter 4) or as a basis for written journaling.

Reflection Activity

Consider answering these questions on a regular basis throughout the internship:

1. What did you experience? To be most effective in this process, you should fully describe, as objectively as possible, such things as meetings, tasks completed, conversations, services you delivered, and others.
2. What did you observe about yourself, other people, policies, written materials, and the physical environment during your experience?
3. What did your experience and observations cause you to think about? Use the following perspectives to guide your reflection.
   • How might my experiences be perceived by students?
   • How might my experiences be interpreted by staff?
   • How might my experiences be seen by other members of the community (e.g., faculty, administrators, members of the public)?
4. What do existing theories or research tell me about my experience?
5. How do my emotions, values, experiences, and preferences impact how I interpret my experience?
6. What tentative conclusions or hypotheses can I draw from my experience, observations, or reflections?
7. What actions do I need to take or what questions do I need to ask to either strengthen or disprove my tentative conclusions?

Learning Preferences and Effects on Internships

When thinking back to the cases of Marcia and Elliott at the beginning of the chapter, it is clear that neither would have maximized their learning and progress toward becoming an intentional student affairs practitioner—unless they incorporated a more flexible and balanced approach, incorporating approaches that are different from what is intuitive or comfortable. Kolb's (1981) theory can guide this process of integrating highly disparate learning styles and preferences into a powerful supervised practice experience.

To be fully open to concrete experience, for example, requires that one suspend the analysis associated with the abstract conceptualization phase. To be truly reflective requires that one refrain from the action and risk taking specified in the active experimentation stage. To be effective in completing the learning cycle requires that one move from observer to actor and from active involvement in the experience to the detachment needed to analyze and draw conclusions about the experience. Kolb (1981) contended that individuals, because of their life experience and current environment, tend to prefer some learning activities more than others. That is, individuals choose the ways they prefer to take in information, either through concrete experience or abstract conceptualization. They also choose their preference for processing information, either through reflective observation or active experimentation (Evans, Forney, Guido, Patton, & Renn, 2010).

The Kolb (1981) typology describes four different learning styles. As we have already discussed, failing to understand one's preferred learning style and failing to strengthen one's less preferred learning abilities can prevent fully realizing opportunities offered by the supervised practice experience. For example, suppose that Carlos and Caroline are both interns in the community standards office. This office is very busy, with an increasing number of student conduct cases. Interns are expected to participate in a brief orientation designed to teach them the procedural information they need to share with students accused of conduct code violations. At the close of this orientation, interns are expected to begin sharing this procedural information with accused students. Caroline is pleased because she has learned exactly what to say to students whom she will encounter in this office. She now knows the nuts-and-bolts steps she should follow. Carlos, on the other hand, is highly critical of the orientation because he has gained little understanding of why students get into trouble and what models he can use to encourage them to avoid violating conduct code rules. Carlos feels unready to begin direct work with students.

Kolb (1981) described four types of learners: (a) convergers, (b) divergers, (c) assimilators, and (d) accommodators. *Convergers'* greatest learning abilities are abstract conceptualization and active experimentation. They prefer technical tasks to interpersonal concerns and like to be involved in problem solving, decision making, and the application of ideas. Caroline could be classified as a converger given her comfort level in interpreting procedural information to students accused of code violations. *Divergers* are most adept at concrete experience and observation and reflection. In other words, they are the direct opposites of the convergers. They tend to be highly imaginative, enjoy observing and reflecting, and can generate multiple alternative solutions to a problem. They tend to enjoy interacting with others and are interested in understanding others' feelings. *Assimilators*, whose strengths are in abstract conceptualization and observation and reflection, focus on ideas rather than people. They tend to evaluate the quality of ideas based on logic rather than practicality. They, also, have the ability to create theories by integrating ideas. In the earlier example, Carlos could be classified as an assimilator. He was uncomfortable explaining procedures to students because he had not been provided with the models (theoretical underpinnings) that guided those procedures. *Accommodators* are action-oriented individuals who are adept at concrete experience and active experimentation. They rely on information from others rather than theories, tend to be adaptable in new situations, solve problems intuitively, and are at ease in group decision making.

Applying Kolb's (1984) theory to one's learning experience as an intern requires a great deal of flexibility and self-knowledge. The first step is to have a clear understanding of one's learning preferences. The brief descriptions mentioned previously as well as the information about Kolb's theory provided in Kolb (1981) and Evans et al. (2010) can help one begin this process. Once interns have a better sense of their preferred learning style, they can begin to target those learning tasks that will likely be more challenging.

The Case of Patsy

Suppose that Patsy, a master's student in college student affairs administration, is starting her first internship in the community service office of a community college near her university. Similar to many student affairs master's students, Patsy's preferred learning style is that of accommodator (Forney, 1994). She likes action and new experiences, so her interactions with potential student volunteers are comfortable and interesting to her.

One of the projects she has undertaken is to create a comprehensive manual for organizations wishing to engage in community service. This project will require gathering manuals from other universities and colleges, analyzing the contents of these manuals, reflecting on the best way to present the information, and determining how to make the manual useful to the students at this community college. This project is not one that particularly interests Patsy initially because it requires more reflection, observation, and technical problem solving than she typically prefers. As she proceeds with the project, she relies more on conversations with student affairs professionals at other schools who have created the manuals rather than on her own ability to analyze. Because she does not spend much time thinking through ways to adapt the manuals to the local student clientele that includes many nontraditional students, her supervisor believes the completed manual was inadequate.

If Patsy had taken the time to adapt her learning style to the requirements for completing the tasks before her, it is likely that she would have produced a more acceptable manual. Patsy would have been well advised to spend time reflecting on her work at various stages in the development of the manual and critiquing it from the perspective of a student enrolled in that community college. In other words, Patsy should have challenged herself to engage in the learning activities preferred by convergers, divergers, and assimilators. (It could have been helpful for Patsy to have sought out others, students or staff, with different learning styles to critique her plan for the manual.)

Kolb (1984) argued that to be an effective learner throughout one's life span, one must integrate disparate learning styles into a flexible approach that recognizes the importance of context and creative approaches to problem solving. Yet learning to integrate one's less preferred learning styles and to adapt one's style to the context of the supervised learning experience requires time, energy, and insight into one's strengths and weaknesses. Typically, when students are asked to adapt their learning styles, they are uncomfortable, less confident, and require more support from others in the setting. The next Reflection Activity is designed to help interns integrate their internship tasks with their learning style.

Reflection Activity

1. Using Kolb's theory as a guide and incorporating information from newer adult learning theories, describe your learning style. Identify strengths and weaknesses of this style. Give examples of ways in which your learning style has, in the past year, facilitated or impeded your progress toward accomplishing important activities.

2. Take a look back at the questions in the first Reflection Activity in this chapter, especially question 4. After reflecting on your learning style according to Kolb's theory and its impact on your accomplishment of important activities, would you like to modify your earlier response to this question? What modifications might you like to make? Why?

Starting Learning in the Supervised Practice Experience

Maximizing learning in supervised practice requires a clear understanding of the desired outcomes from the experience and use of a conceptual framework, such as Kolb's theory. Starting a supervised practice experience in a positive manner is another fundamental component of maximizing learning. In this section we outline a number of important considerations as one begins supervised practice.

Depending on the nature of the experience and requirements of a preparation program or particular office, matching a student with a supervised experience site can take a variety of forms. There might be a formal, highly competitive application and selection process with carefully structured documentation, or the student and site supervisor might simply agree to work together. Regardless of the nature of this matching process, an intern who desires to gain maximum learning from the experience needs to gather considerable information and understanding early in the internship. Although many supervisors provide orientation information, it is also important that students take the initiative to learn specifics about the office, its culture, and its expectations. This type of contextual information will provide a much-needed framework for the learning that will take place on site. Also, understanding the office and the way the office works will prevent early missteps that might compromise the intern's credibility and thereby thwart some opportunities for learning. Following are some actions to take at the outset of a supervised practice experience to create optimal learning conditions.

Become Familiar with Written Documents

- *Carefully read the public statements about the organization's mission, vision, and strategic plan.* These can often be found on office websites, but if not, it is essential that a new graduate student ask for these documents. It is important that one understands what the office presents to the public as its purpose and priorities.
- *Examine assessment documents that describe the characteristics of students who are served by the organization or the effectiveness of particular programs.* There are a variety of ways to understand the student population served by an organization. Certainly conversations with students or observations of their interactions with an office are important. But it is easy to overlook assessment data and reports as a source of understanding. Most offices collect information about who uses the particular programs and may even disaggregate these data by racial, ethnic, gender-identity, and sexual-orientation groups. The results of satisfaction surveys, while not the only source that can be used to understand effectiveness, can help the intern begin to think about the ways in which the office meets students' needs.
- *If there is a written description of the internship responsibilities and opportunities, read it carefully enough to know the fine details.* In the excitement of preparing for work with students or other constituencies, it can be easy to forget the specifics of the position description. Or it might be tempting to gloss over points of the description that are confusing for fear of appearing inept. Start the internship experience with a clear understanding of the position requirements.
- *If the organization has procedural manuals or reference guides related to the scope of the intern's responsibilities, read them at the start of the supervised practice experience.* Being familiar with relevant internship site procedures early in the experience can build confidence and credibility. Suppose, for example, that Sally is doing a semester-long internship in the College of Business advising center. If Sally develops expertise about the course

requirements, sequence of courses, and regulations about academic standards in the first week of the term, it is likely she will be able to provide direct student services more quickly. Also, she will be able to demonstrate her initiative and professionalism to her site supervisor and colleagues in a tangible way.

Exploring the Organizational Work Culture

- *Observe or ask questions about basic norms of professional life in a particular site.* Although understanding any organizational culture is best accomplished over time and with sustained interaction, it is possible to get glimpses at the outset of the supervised practice experience. For example, an intern can observe or ask about the dress that is expected for professional staff. Whether staff use their formal titles (e.g., Dr., Ms., Mr.) with students or colleagues is important to know as the internship begins. It is perfectly appropriate to ask a supervisor how they and others would like to be addressed. If it is not possible to ask directly, it is better to be too formal rather than too casual.
- *Become familiar with organizational relationships.* One can glean a great deal of information about organizational dynamics by simply reading the organizational chart. It is also important to discuss who reports to whom and how the organization relates to the college or university, since there may be nuances that are not apparent in the written documents. With some office staffs, the supervisor manages the workflow; with others, the lines of authority and responsibility are more ambiguous. As another example, there are some offices where administrative assistants are tasked (either formally or informally) with supporting the work of interns and others where it would be completely inappropriate for an intern to ask for help from an administrative assistant. Discussing the actual roles and responsibilities of the staff members is often a helpful activity at the outset of the internship.

Getting Mentally Prepared for Learning

- *Recognize that a supervised practice experience has a relatively short duration.* In the lives of organizations such as colleges and universities, a staff member who is present for an academic term or even through a two-year master's program can be considered a short-timer. Creating impactful programs and initiatives often takes much longer. For example, a summer-term intern tasked with designing a fall-semester residence hall roommate conflict-prevention workshop will never actually see how the program works or how it can be improved for the second iteration. Interns may not be given certain responsibilities, like supervision of paraprofessional staff, simply because they cannot develop the supervisory relationship during the short duration of their internship. Recognizing the short-term nature of supervised practice experiences at the outset is essential for creating reasonable goals and plans.

• *Plan to think deeply about what is observed and experienced.* Internships are different from professional experiences in a variety of ways; one of the most important is the emphasis on learning knowledge, skills, and attitudes that can be generalized to contexts beyond the internship. Task completion in an internship is fundamentally a means to an end: students' learning. If the intern focuses solely on the doing of the internship—planning programs, facilitating trainings, or advising students, for example—meaningful learning can certainly be diminished. At the outset of a supervised practice experience, it is important to build in adequate time and support for reflection—with supervisors, with colleagues, or alone. Interns should allow both time and mental energy for thinking about why certain things happen in an office or how what one studies in a class plays out in practice.

References

American College Personnel Association. (2006). *Statement of ethical principles and standards.* Retrieved from www.myacpa.org/au/documents/EthicsStatement.pdf

American College Personnel Association (ACPA)/National Association of Student Affairs Administrators (NASPA). (2010). *Professional competency areas for student affairs practitioners.* Washington, DC: American College Personnel Association and National Association of Student Personnel Administrators.

American Council on Education. (1937). *The student personnel point of view.* Retrieved from www.myacpa.org/pub/documents/1937.pdf

Baxter Magolda, M. B., & King, P. M. (Eds.). (2004). *Learning partnerships: Theory and models of practice to educate for self-authorship.* Sterling, VA: Stylus.

Council for the Advancement of Standards in Higher Education (CAS). (2012). *CAS professional standards for higher education* (8th ed.). Washington, DC: Author.

Creamer, D. G., Winston, R. B., Jr., & Miller, T. K. (2001). The professional student affairs administrator: Roles and functions. In R. B. Winston, Jr., D. G. Creamer, T. K. Miller, & Associates (Eds.), *The professional student affairs administrator: Educator, leader, and manager* (pp. 3–38). Philadelphia, PA: Brunner-Rutledge.

Cuyjet, M., Longwell-Grice, R., & Molina, E. (2009). Perceptions of new student affairs professionals and their supervisors regarding the application of competencies learned in preparation programs. *Journal of College Student Development, 50*(1), 104–119.

Damasio, A. (1999). *The feeling of what happens: Body and emotion in the making of consciousness.* New York, NY: Harcourt Brace.

Delworth, U., & Hanson, G. R. (1980). Conclusion: Structure of the profession and recommended curriculum. In U. Delworth, G. R. Hanson, & Associates (Eds.), *Student services: A handbook for the profession* (pp. 473–485). San Francisco, CA: Jossey-Bass.

Dirkx, J. M. (2001). The power of feelings: Emotion, imagination, and the construction of meaning in adult learning. *New Directions for Adult and Continuing Education, 2001*(89), 63–72. doi:10.1002/ace.9

Evans, N., Forney, D. S., Guido, F. M., Patton, L. D., Renn, K. A. (2010). *Student development in college: Theory, research, and practice.* San Francisco, CA: Jossey Bass.

Evans, N. J., & Guido, F. M. (2012). Response to Patrick Love's "informal theory": A rejoinder. *Journal of College Student Development, 53*(2), 192–200.

Forney, D. S. (1994). A profile of student affairs master's students: Characteristics, attitudes, and learning styles. *Journal of College Student Development, 35*(4), 337–345.

Fried, J. (1997). Changing ethical frameworks for a multicultural world. In J. Fried (Ed.), *Ethics for today's campus: New perspectives on education, student development, and institutional management* (pp. 5–22). New Directions for Student Services, No. 77. San Francisco, CA: Jossey-Bass.

Fried, J. (2011). Ethical standards and principles. In J. H. Schuh, S. R. Jones, & S. R. Harper (Eds.), *Student services: A handbook for the profession* (pp. 96–119). San Francisco, CA: Jossey Bass.

Greenleaf, E. A. (1977). Preparation of student personnel staff to meet flexibility and diversity in higher education. In G. H. Knock (Ed.), *Perspectives on the preparation of student affairs professionals* (pp. 155–165). Student Personnel Series, No. 22. Washington, DC: American College Personnel Association.

Herdlein, R. (2004). Survey of chief student affairs professionals regarding relevance of graduate preparation programs. *NASPA Journal, 42*(1), 51–71.

Hill, L. H. (2001). The brain and consciousness: Sources of information for understanding adult learning. *New Directions for Adult and Continuing Education, 2001*(89), 73–82. doi:10.1002/ace.10

Jones, S. R., & Abes, E. (2011). The nature and uses of theory. In J. H. Schuh, S. R. Jones, & S. R. Harper (Eds.), *Student services: A handbook for the profession* (pp. 149–167). San Francisco, CA: Jossey Bass.

Knock, G. H. (Ed.). (1977). *Perspectives on the preparation of student affairs professionals.* Student Personnel Series, No. 22. Washington, DC: American College Personnel Association.

Kolb, D. A. (1981). Learning styles and disciplinary differences. In A. W. Chickering (Ed.), *The modern American college: Responding to the new realities of diverse students and a changing society* (pp. 232–255). San Francisco, CA: Jossey Bass.

Kolb, D. A. (1984). *Experiential learning: Experience as the source of learning and development.* Englewood Cliffs, NJ: Prentice Hall.

Kuh, G. D., & Whitt, E. J. (1988). *The invisible tapestry: Culture in American colleges and universities.* ASHE/ERIC Higher Education Report, No. 1. Washington, DC: Association for the Study of Higher Education.

Lampkin, P. (2007). Educating the whole student in 2007. *Vermont Connection, 28*, 137–142.

Levine, A., & Dean D. (2012). *Generation on a tightrope: A portrait of today's college student.* San Francisco, CA: Jossey Bass.

Love, P. (2012). Informal theory: The ignored link in theory-to-practice. *Journal of College Student Development, 53*(2), 177–191.

Lovell, C., & Kosten, L. (2000). Skills, knowledge, and personal traits necessary for success as a student affairs administrator: A meta-analysis of thirty years of research. *NASPA Journal, 37*(4), 553–572.

Magolda, P. M., & Baxter Magolda, M. B. (2011). Engaging in dialogues about difference in the workplace. In P. M. Magolda & M. B. Baxter Magolda (Eds.), *Contested issues in student affairs: Diverse perspectives and respectful dialogues* (pp. 453–465). Sterling, VA: Stylus.

McEwen, M. L. & Talbot, D. M. (1977). Designing the student affairs curriculum. In N. J. Evans & C. E. Phelps-Tobin (Eds.), *The state of the art of preparation and practice in student affairs: Another look* (pp. 125–156). Lanham, MD: University Press of America.

McGlothlin, W. J. (1964). *The professional schools.* New York, NY: Center for Applied Research in Education.

Merriam, S. B., Caffarella, R. S., & Baumgartner, L. M. (2006). *Learning in adulthood: A comprehensive guide* (3rd ed.). San Francisco, CA: Jossey Bass.

Nash, R. (1997). Teaching ethics in the student affairs classroom. *NASPA Journal, 35*(1), 3–19.

Pope, R. L., Reynolds, A. L., & Mueller, J. A. (2004). *Multicultural competence in student affairs.* San Francisco, CA: Jossey Bass.

Reber, A. S. (1993*). Implicit learning and tacit knowledge: An essay on the cognitive unconscious.* Oxford Psychological Series, No. 19. New York, NY: Oxford University Press.

Renn, K., & Hodges, J. (2007). In the first year on the job: Experiences of new professionals. *NASPA Journal, 44*(2), 367–391.

Roberts, D. (2012). The 1937 Student Personnel Point of View as a catalyst for 75 years of dialogue. *Journal of College Student Development, 53*(1), 2–18.

Saunders, S. A., & Cooper, D. L. (1999). The doctorate in student affairs: Competencies and skills for mid-management. *Journal of College Student Development, 40*(2), 185–191.

Saunders, S. A., & Lease Butts, J. (2011). Teaching integrity. In R. B. Young (Ed.), *Advancing the integrity of professional practice* (pp. 67–78). New Directions for Student Services, No. 135. San Francisco, CA: Jossey Bass.

Selingo, J. J. (2013). *College unbound: The future of higher education and what it means for students.* Boston, MA: Houghton-Mifflin Harcourt.

Sheckley, B. G., & Bell, A. (2006). Experience, consciousness, and learning: Implications for instruction. In S. Johnson & K. Taylor (Eds.), *Neuroscience of adult learning* (pp. 43–52). New Directions for Adult and Continuing Education, No. 110. Somerset, NJ: Wiley & Sons.

Sheckley, B. G., & Keeton, M. T. (2001). *Improving employee development: Perspectives from research and practice.* Chicago, IL: Council for the Adult and Experiential Learning.

Waple, N. J. (2006). An assessment of skills and competencies necessary for entry-level student affairs work. *NASPA Journal, 43*(1), 1–18.

Winston, R. B., Jr., & Saunders, S. A. (1991). Ethical professional practice in student affairs. In T. K. Miller, R. B. Winston, Jr., & Associates (Eds.), *Administration and leadership in student affairs: Actualizing student development in higher education* (2nd ed., pp. 309–345). Muncie, IN: Accelerated Development.

2 Structure and Design of the Internship

Historically, supervised practice or internships have played an essential role in the preparation of student affairs practitioners. Most graduate preparation programs have offered such experiences for decades, and they are generally viewed as a fundamental component of the curriculum (Winston et al., 2001). Indeed, as discussed in Chapter 1, supervised practice experiences are a core component of the CAS master's-level preparation standards (Miller, 2001).

When intentionally designed and clearly focused, supervised practice experiences can be one of the most powerful learning and socialization tools for aspiring professionals (Sherman & Crum, 2009). Students can gain personal insights into the operation of an office on campus and hone their skills in a variety of contexts (Saunders & Cooper, 2001). Site supervisors have an opportunity to pass along their expertise about a functional area for which they have proven track records. Faculty members are able to assist students in translating classroom instruction to professional practice.

On the other hand, when such experiences are not clearly defined, this can limit the amount of learning that occurs and can be frustrating for students, supervisors, and faculty. The key to maximizing the effectiveness of an internship, then, is in the design of that experience (McCormick, 1993). Featherman (1998) argues that as higher education has become a mature industry, it has undergone a transformation that has resulted in an increased emphasis on service and learning through that service. Others have identified more specific outcomes associated with such experiences. For example, Carter, Cooke, and Neal (1996) suggest that internships should enable students to make and justify decisions, plan and control activities, evaluate the results of activities, communicate effectively, work with people effectively, and continue their personal development (p. 66). Other specific objectives of field experiences include research, career exploration, community service, and intercultural experience. These are not necessarily mutually exclusive, and they can be combined when designing an internship (Murphy & Kaffenberger, 2007).

The consensus of many scholars is that internships should offer students insights into the world of work, develop professional skills, develop interpersonal and social skills, link theory to practice, and enhance employment prospects for students (Carter et al., 1996; Narayanan, Olk, & Fukami, 2010;

Ryan & Cassidy, 1996; Toohey, Ryan, & Hughes, 1996). Internships should also socialize students in the professional roles to which they aspire (Fender & Watson, 2005; Sherman & Crum, 2009) and allow them to integrate theory, research, practice (Beenen & Rousseau, 2010), and to develop professional values (Delve, Mintz, & Stewart, 1990).

Even though these shared objectives may be applicable to a variety of supervised practice experiences, some are related to discussions of undergraduate internship experiences, and others come from disciplines such as psychology, business, or clinical counseling. In this chapter, we emphasize how supervised experiences can be designed to maximize learning for those aspiring to careers in student affairs administration. To this end, we recommend a model for designing successful internship experiences in higher education that consists of six components:

- Conducting a personal skills assessment
- Setting realistic expectations
- Developing a contract for the experience
- Understanding the roles and the pedagogy of the experience
- Identifying the resources necessary to conduct the experience
- Balancing the experience with other curriculum components and student lives

Each of these six components is addressed in this chapter, but it is important for students to note that they need not design the internship without assistance and direction. The faculty member who coordinates the internship program is an invaluable resource to students planning supervised experiences. We encourage students to consult with their faculty supervisors throughout the planning process (see Chapter 3 for a discussion of the roles of the on-site and faculty supervisors).

Conducting a Personal Skills Assessment

Given the extensive literature about supervised experiences, there is surprisingly little written about assessing students' skills prior to the internship. Those seeking internships frequently simply identify basic skills they might bring to the experience, such as technical, clerical, organizational, or artistic skills (Green, 1997). This type of minimalist approach to assessment is not likely to result in an experience specifically designed to improve skills.

The internship should be carefully and purposively designed if students expect to maximize learning from the experience. This requires students to conduct a thorough assessment of the skills they bring to potential sites, *and* the skills they believe they need to improve to develop their professional craft. This assessment should be sufficiently broad in scope to enable the student to see potential gains that could be achieved in any number of settings. If students examine only the skills required to succeed in a single setting, they limit the potential that a given internship may afford. If students consider skills in a broad array of areas, they may identify a number of potential sites where supervised practice could contribute to personal and professional development.

The two major professional associations in student affairs have identified 10 competencies that are essential to successful practice (American College Personnel Association [ACPA]/National Association of Student Affairs Administrators [NASPA], 2010). These include the following:

1. *Advising and Helping.* The Advising and Helping competency area addresses the knowledge, skills, and attitudes related to providing counseling and advising support, direction, feedback, critique, referral, and guidance to individuals and groups (p. 7).

2. *Assessment, Evaluation, and Research.* The Assessment, Evaluation, and Research competency area (AER) focuses on the ability to use, design, conduct, and critique qualitative and quantitative AER analyses; to manage organizations using AER processes and the results obtained from them; and to shape the political and ethical climate surrounding AER processes and uses on campus (p. 10).

3. *Equity, Diversity, and Inclusion.* The Equity, Diversity, and Inclusion (EDI) competency area includes the knowledge, skills, and attitudes needed to create learning environments that are enriched with diverse views and people. It is also designed to create an institutional ethos that accepts and celebrates differences among people, helping to free them of any misconceptions and prejudices (p. 12).

4. *Ethical Professional Practice.* The Ethical Professional Practice competency area pertains to the knowledge, skills, and attitudes needed to understand and apply ethical standards to one's work. While ethics is an integral component of all the competency areas, this competency area focuses specifically on the integration of ethics into all aspects of self- and professional practice (p. 14).

5. *History, Philosophy, and Values.* The History, Philosophy, and Values competency area involves knowledge, skills, and attitudes that connect the history, philosophy, and values of the profession to one's current professional practice. This competency area embodies the foundations of the profession from which current and future research and practice will grow. The commitment to demonstrating this competency area ensures that our present and future practices are informed by an understanding of our history, philosophy, and values (p. 16).

6. *Human and Organizational Resources.* The Human and Organizational Resources competency area includes knowledge, skills, and attitudes used in the selection, supervision, motivation, and formal evaluation of staff; conflict resolution; management of the politics of organizational discourse; and the effective application of strategies and techniques associated with financial resources, facilities management, fundraising, technology use, crisis management, risk management, and sustainable resources (p. 18).

7. *Law, Policy, and Governance.* The Law, Policy, and Governance competency area includes the knowledge, skills, and attitudes relating to policy development processes used in various contexts, the application of legal constructs, and the understanding of governance structures and their impact on one's professional practice (p. 21).
8. *Leadership.* The Leadership competency area addresses the knowledge, skills, and attitudes required of a leader, whether it be a positional leader or a member of the staff, in both an individual capacity and within a process of how individuals work together effectively to envision, plan, effect change in organizations, and respond to internal and external constituencies and issues (p. 21).
9. *Personal Foundations.* The Personal Foundations competency area involves the knowledge, skills, and attitudes to maintain emotional, physical, social, environmental, relational, spiritual, and intellectual wellness; be self-directed and self-reflective; maintain excellence and integrity in work; be comfortable with ambiguity; be aware of one's own areas of strength and growth; have a passion for work; and remain curious (p. 26).
10. *Student Learning and Development.* The Student Learning and Development competency area addresses the concepts and principles of student development and learning theory. This includes the ability to apply theory to improve and inform student affairs practice, as well as understanding teaching and training theory and practice (p. 28).

Although there may be other areas that should be assessed by those considering an internship (for instance, technology), the 10 areas of expertise described here comprise a sound basis for students to assess their knowledge and skills. Moreover, the way in which the assessment is conducted is important if the supervised experience is to be intentionally designed. That is, it is important for students to assess their current levels of skill in each of the 10 areas, but it is equally important to assess how significant each area is to their professional aspirations. For those who seek careers in admissions, for example, developing advising and helping skills to promote relationships with nontraditional students might be more important than developing skills in human and organizational resources. Others who seek careers in residential life, student activities, or fraternity or sorority life may find developing leadership skills more important to their immediate professional goals. In the long run, however, developing skills in all 10 areas is essential for professional advancement. Indeed, there may be other skills that students seek to develop through supervised experiences. If so, they should make a concerted effort to design an internship that will enable them to develop those talents (Stewart, 1994). Students also should keep in mind that because of changing personal interests, societal expectations and demands, and personal circumstances, it is difficult to accurately envision a career path at this stage of development.

In addition to identifying competency areas that all professionals should possess, ACPA and NASPA developed lists of specific basic, intermediate, and advanced skills that professionals should hone in each of the 10 areas. The ACPA/NASPA Professional Competency Areas Basic Skills Self-Assessment (BSSA) appears in Appendix 1. It consists of 125 items that students can use to identify skills they wish to work on in any given practicum setting. Additionally, the instrument calls on respondents to rate the extent to which they hope to develop each skill by the time they complete the graduate program. Those who have identified other skills they would like to develop through their internships might create additional questions such as those found on the BSSA relevant to those additional skills.

By completing the inventory, students create a profile of current skill levels and skills to be acquired before completing the program of study. Using the resulting profile enables students to critically evaluate their options with respect to supervised practice experiences. Given their understanding, students can design supervised experiences that enable them to work on some of the skills that they believe they will need to succeed as professionals. This assessment provides the groundwork needed to consider the next component of the design process, setting realistic expectations.

Reflection Activity

Turn to Appendix 1 and complete the BSSA for either the internship you are currently in or one you hope to complete in the future. Once you have rated your current and desired skill levels, think about the following questions:

1. Given your career interest(s), what three competency areas are the most important for you to work on?
2. Given what you know about yourself, what competency areas will be the most challenging for you to develop?
3. For those challenging areas, what behaviors can you engage in to develop your expertise and skills?

Setting Realistic Expectations

Once students have an understanding of their current abilities and the skills they wish to hone while in graduate school, the next step in designing the supervised experience is to set realistic expectations for that experience. Those who successfully complete internships are more likely to be deemed qualified for entry-level positions than those who have not worked in a professional setting. They are also more likely to report greater satisfaction with their positions and to earn higher salaries than those who did not complete a supervised experience (Taylor, 1992). These expectations are not likely to be achieved, however, if the experience is not intentionally designed.

It is likely that the assessment process revealed a number of skills that students have already developed fairly fully. That process is also likely to have identified a number of skills that students have not yet developed but that will be important to their future success as practitioners. It is unrealistic to expect that any given internship experience is going to enable students to develop all the skills they will need as professionals. Indeed, it is important to consider all the mechanisms available to students to develop the skills they will need to succeed in the profession.

For example, skills can be developed through other classes offered in the graduate curriculum. If students want to develop skills that enable them to understand student learning and development, they might use assignments from a class on cognitive or student development theory to sharpen their skills. Students seeking to develop human and organizational resource management skills might take advantage of assignments in a staff supervision class to gain that expertise and those skills. Those who wish to develop research abilities may enroll in a research design class that would enable them to focus on developing a research project on a topic of their choosing. The point is that students can develop their skills through didactic-type classes as well as internships.

A second opportunity to practice and enhance skills is provided in graduate assistantship positions (GAs). Many graduate preparation programs in higher education and student affairs administration work with other campus administrators to offer students GA positions. These positions can be in any number of offices, including admissions, financial aid, academic advising, career services, housing and dining services, student activities, or judicial affairs, among others. In exchange for working 10–20 hours per week in a given office, students in GA positions are provided a stipend and, in some cases, tuition remission. Many administrators and students view GA positions as a way of funding graduate education, and in fact, GA positions are a form of financial support for graduate students. But GA experiences go beyond merely funding a student's graduate education. They are opportunities for students to develop and practice skills they will need in their professional careers. In that sense, GA positions can serve as mechanisms for students to hone their skills, and students should use these opportunities accordingly. (Review Chapter 1 for a discussion of the assistantship and similarities and differences between it and the internship.)

Finally, it is important for students to consider opportunities to develop skills that may be better addressed outside the classroom or internship. Professional associations are a prime example of such opportunities. Most professional associations in higher education and student affairs administration offer reduced membership rates for graduate students, and we urge students to take advantage of those rates to further their professional development. Joining associations not only provides students with regular member benefits, such as receiving journals and other publications, but it also offers students opportunities to develop other professional skills. For example, those who wish to develop ethical professional practice skills may decide to submit proposals to present programs at professional gatherings on current ethical issues. Students who wish to gain experience in leadership might volunteer to serve on a committee responsible for developing an association's annual conference. The point is that there are opportunities to learn professional skills beyond those offered through formal supervised practice courses. Since it is unlikely that any internship will provide students with opportunities to address all the skills they would like to develop, it is incumbent upon students to make use of all the opportunities the graduate education process provides them. In this manner, students are more likely to have their expectations of professional preparation fully met.

Respondents to the BSSA (ACPA/NASPA, 2010) are asked to identify the skills they most want to develop through a single supervised experience. This list of skills and concomitant knowledge areas can then be used to identify a site that might promote the development of such skills to the greatest extent. For example, suppose that the student has identified the following as the skills she or he would most prefer to work on during the experience: identifying the contributions of similar and diverse people within and to the institutional environment (for instance, Hispanic students to White students); using technological resources to maximize the efficiency and effectiveness of one's work; facilitating dialogue effectively among disparate audiences; and facilitating appropriate data collection for system- or department-wide assessment and evaluation efforts using up-to-date technology and methods. The next step in the process is to identify one or more supervised experiences that would provide opportunities to work on these skills. There may be several options for the student to combine the development of these skills.

One option would be to work with a campus multicultural center on a project to incorporate Hispanic student events into a campus calendar. This would enable the intern to identify the contributions of Hispanics to the campus environment and, by incorporating their plans into other campus activities, to facilitate dialogue among disparate audiences. Such an experience might also enable the intern to use technological resources when gathering information for the calendar. Such an internship would enable the student to gain experience related to three of the four skills identified in the assessment process. The final skill area, facilitate appropriate data collection, could then be addressed in another supervised practice setting or through other curricular avenues.

Another option for a student seeking to develop skills in these four areas would be an assignment in a service learning center. Perhaps the intern could work with a group of undergraduates who serve as tutors for disadvantaged high school students. Such an assignment might require the intern to conduct an initial assessment of the high school students' skills (facilitating data collection) and represent their interests to the student tutors (identify contributions of a group). This experience might meet two of the four designated goals for the experience. In this case, facilitating dialogue among diverse groups and using technology to maximize efficiency and effectiveness might have to be postponed, but the intern's other objectives could be met.

Finally, there may be an internship that could address all four objectives. Consider the opportunities that an office that serves students with disabilities provides. Interns may design an experience that would allow them to advise the Students with Disabilities Club on how to get a webpage created. The intern would start by learning about the contributions of this group to the campus environment so he or she would know what the page should contain. To do so, the intern would conduct an assessment of the organization's needs (collect appropriate data), assist the students in developing the information needed for the page (using technology to maximize effectiveness), and help the students determine the budget needed to hire a Web designer. Finally, the intern could facilitate a conversation between club members and student government officers to request the funding needed for the project. Such an experience would provide opportunities for all four of the intern's objectives to be met.

These three examples suggest representative activities in which students may engage through an internship. They also typify ways in which students can target the development of certain skills when designing supervised experiences. Students, however, need to be realistic when designing internships. Students are well served if they identify a limited number of realistic goals and intentionally design experiences to achieve those goals. They are less well served if they try to accomplish so many goals through a single experience that they are unable to fully develop any of the skills they seek to cultivate. Once realistic goals for the experience have been identified, the next step in the process is to design the contract for the experience.

Developing a Contract for the Experience

The learning contract represents the clearest expression of what the student hopes to achieve in a supervised experience, what the student plans to bring to the site, and what the student expects the site to contribute to the experience. As a result, developing the contract is an essential component of designing a meaningful internship. Interestingly, few scholars have addressed the issue of the contract when writing about the internship experience. Those who have mentioned the contract have done so in the context that the contract serves as a way of tracking where students are serving, not necessarily what they are doing (Ciofalo, 1992; Dye & Bender, 2006; Mason, 1985; Schmidt, Gardner, Benjamin, Conaway, & Haskins, 1992). Others refer to the contract only tangentially in reference to evaluating the supervised experience (Alexander, 1982; Toohey et al., 1996; Winston et al., 2001). We argue that designing the contract is an essential and important learning activity. When done well, developing the contract should enable students to clearly identify goals, create activities that directly link to those goals, and calculate the amount of time it will take to complete those activities. All these actions allow students to practice planning and time management skills—skills they will need to succeed as professionals.

The Case of Jane

For purposes of discussing the development of the contract, consider the following scenario. Jane has completed the BSSA (ACPA/NASPA, 2010) and has selected five goals that she would like to achieve through an internship.

1. Jane would like to develop her research abilities, particularly those related to reviewing and interpreting literature (Research, Assessment, and Evaluation).
2. She would also like to facilitate problem solving (Advising and Helping).
3. She is interested in gaining experience in linking theory to practice (Student Learning and Development).
4. Jane also wants to gain an understanding of the policies and procedures that guide the judicial process on campus (Law, Policy, and Governance).
5. She desires to learn about the overall operation of the Dean of Students Office, including creating job descriptions, hiring, and supervising (Human and Organizational Resources).

Given these interests, she met with the designated internship supervisor in the Dean of Students Office and, with his assistance, identified a possible internship. Now she needs to develop the contract for that experience.

A good contract will include eight basic elements: student information; site supervisor information; practicum faculty coordinator information; purpose statement; objectives, activities skills or competencies, and time requirements; site location information; proposed work schedule; and signatures. Some of these elements are more informational while others are instructive in tone. All the elements are important to a complete contract and are highly recommended to those planning internships. Each is discussed in the text that follows. We have included a sample contract reflecting Jane's scenario in Appendix 2 to provide an example of what a final contract might look like.

The first three elements are informational items. There are three key people involved in the supervised experience: the student, the site supervisor who provides day-to-day supervision to the student, and the faculty supervisor who coordinates the course associated with the practicum. Since all three need to interact on a regular basis, it is important that the learning contract include each person's role and their contact information, including title, mailing address, office phone, fax number, and e-mail address. Additionally, it might be useful for the student to provide a home address, phone number, and e-mail address because students are not always available during regular business hours.

The purpose statement is an instructive element. It is designed to provide all the parties involved in the experience with a clear, concise overview of what the student intends to do and hopes to achieve from the experience. In Jane's case, the purpose statement suggests that she will conduct research to develop a conflict resolution model that might be used in the adjudication of conduct cases.

She also hopes to gain insight into the overall operation of the dean of students office. Jane has included three of the skills she hopes to develop as a result of the experience in the purpose statement (research, student conflicts, overall operation of the office). This is generally a good idea. First, it serves to remind Jane of what she wants to focus on during the course of the internship. Second, it assists the site supervisor and faculty supervisor in tracking the progress Jane is making toward achieving her objectives during the academic term.

Objectives, activities, skills or competencies, and time, the fifth element of the contract, is another instructive component and represents the substance of the contract. This is the section in which students translate the objectives they hope to achieve during the experience into behaviors in which they will actually engage and estimate how much time they expect to spend on each activity. Because this is such an important element of the contract, each component merits some discussion here. *Objectives* are statements that students develop to describe the general tasks they will perform during the experience. In this sense, they describe outcomes the student hopes to achieve by the conclusion of the internship. Objectives should be clear and easily understood by all parties. In Jane's case, three objectives were identified. First, Jane plans to assist with the development of a conflict resolution model that the dean of students' staff might use in adjudicating certain types of conduct cases. Second, Jane plans to conceptualize the logistics associated with implementing that model. Finally, she hopes to gain an understanding of the overall operation of the dean of students office. In each case, Jane has provided her site supervisor and faculty supervisor with a clear idea of what she plans to accomplish during the internship experience.

The next component, *activities*, is typically the most difficult for students to provide. Activities are descriptions of behaviors in which students will engage to accomplish the objectives cited in the contract. It is critical, therefore, that the activities represent behaviors that, if successfully completed, will lead the student to achieve the relevant objective. Consider Jane's first objective of developing a conflict resolution model. The activities she has identified that are associated with achieving that goal include conducting research on conflict resolution models, consulting with her site supervisor, and conferring with other dean of students' staff members about components of the model. All three activities (behaviors) can be directly connected to the outcome Jane hopes to achieve: developing a conflict resolution model. Moreover, each activity can be related to one of the skills she hopes to develop through the experience. Researching the literature on conflict resolutions relates to her objective of developing her research skills, particularly those associated with interpreting literature. Consulting with her site supervisor and other staff members in the office relates to her objective of understanding the overall function of the office.

In the *skills or competencies* section of the contract, Jane has summarized the skills she believes she will develop as a result of engaging in the activities she has related to her first objective. There are direct connections between the behaviors she will engage in and the skills she will develop as a result of those activities. She notes in this section that she will hone her research skills and collaborate with staff in the office, both skills she might reasonably develop through the activities she has planned.

The final component of this section is frequently the most challenging for students when designing contracts. A good contract will report how much *time* the student plans to spend on each activity. This requires that the student calculate time in as specific a manner as possible. For example, Jane has indicated she plans to spend approximately 15 hours consulting with her site supervisor. In this case, Jane's experience will occur during a 15-week semester. Her estimate suggests she plans to spend 1 hour per week with her site supervisor in individual sessions, a realistic estimate of how much time will be devoted to this activity. The same is true for meeting with other staff members. In this case, there are five other professionals in the office. Jane's plan suggests she will spend 1 hour with each over the course of the semester, a realistic expectation for this portion of the contract. Estimating research time may be more difficult, but by reporting her plan to spend 20 hours on this task, and assuming all research will need to be conducted before she can start on her second objective, conceptualizing the model, Jane is suggesting that she spend about 4 hours per week conducting research during the first five weeks of her experience. In total, Jane estimates she will spend about 40 hours on the activities related to achieving her first objective. These kinds of accurate estimates can be useful to students when they examine all the objectives they hope to achieve in a given experience. In some cases, students identify too few or too many objectives to reasonably achieve in a given academic term. Accurate time estimates help students identify when such problems might occur.

Jane repeated these steps in developing the second and third objectives of her contract. In each case, the activities she has proposed directly relate to the relevant objective. In each case, she has described skills and competencies that she can reasonably assume she can develop if she engages in those activities. Finally, she has allocated time to each activity based on realistic expectations about how much time it will take to complete those activities. She has also indicated the total amount of time she plans to spend in the supervised experience over the course of the academic term. This is an important consideration when developing contracts. Most graduate preparation programs have internal, departmental standards associated with supervised experiences. These standards normally include a specified number of hours students should expect to spend at the site. Students should consult those guidelines when developing contracts so they can design experiences that not only meet their objectives but meet departmental expectations as well.

It is also important to note that Jane has included language in her contract that reflects all five of the objectives she identified through her assessment as important to achieve. Research skills are included in the first objective. Linking theory to practice and problem-solving skills are included in the activities associated with the contract's second objective. Understanding the policies and procedures that guide the judicial process and gaining an understanding of the overall operation of the dean of students office are reflected in the activities associated with the third objective. Overall, then, Jane has designed an experience that will not only provide a valuable service to the site where she will work but will also allow her to acquire skills in the five areas she identified through the assessment process.

The remaining three sections of the contract are instructive elements. In the site location section, students note where they plan to conduct the activities described in the contract. In most cases, the site supervisor will need to provide space for the student. Some activities, such as conducting research, may be conducted at other locations, but it is essential that the student have a space somewhere on-site if the student expects to be a contributing member of the staff.

The proposed work schedule is another important component for all parties involved in the contract. Students need to balance the expectations of the supervised experience with the other obligations they assume each academic term, including other classes, jobs, GA positions, studying time, and personal life. The site supervisor needs to have a general idea of when to expect the student in the office. In many cases, interns share office space with other employees, and the site supervisor may need to juggle various demands on office space to accommodate the student. Knowing when the student plans to work enables the site supervisor to accomplish the necessary planning. Finally, the faculty supervisor will benefit from knowing the proposed schedule. The schedule provides the faculty supervisor with an idea of how much time the student will be spending on site, enabling her or him to evaluate whether the schedule will allow the student to accomplish the objectives of the contract and balance those responsibilities with other academic demands.

The final element is the signatures of the three parties involved in the experience. This may seem like a minor bureaucratic matter, but signatures suggest that all the parties have reviewed the components of the contract and have agreed to the parameters of the contract. It is also important that the student obtain all signatures prior to starting work at the site. If the student is to meet all the time requirements of the contract, this usually means designing the contract and obtaining signatures prior to the start of the academic term in which the student enrolls for the supervised experience. Doing so calls for advance planning on the part of the student. But we would argue that supervised experiences are most meaningful when they are intentionally planned. Intentional planning, including consulting with the site supervisor and identifying clear objectives and activities, requires time that is typically not available to students during the crunch that accompanies the opening weeks of an academic term. Therefore, we encourage students to conduct their assessments and develop their contracts in the weeks preceding the term in which they plan to conduct the experience. Once the contract has been developed and signed, the next step in the process relates to the structure around which the supervised experience is designed.

Understanding the Roles and the Pedagogy of the Experience

Once students have assessed their skills, targeted those they wish to develop, identified a site for the supervised practice, and designed the contract, they often feel that the only remaining element of the experience is to conduct the work. But that is not necessarily the case. It is important to have an understanding of the structure around which that experience will be built. This structure includes two components: the roles those involved in the experience will play and the pedagogical approach the experience assumes.

Roles in the Supervised Experience

There are three key players in every supervised experience: the student, the site supervisor, and the faculty supervisor. Each plays a distinctive role in the experience. Each brings certain expectations to the experience, and each expects certain outcomes from the experience. Understanding a bit about each of those roles may provide insight into how the structure of the experience works. (The roles of the supervisors are dealt with in greater detail in Chapter 3.)

The student is the first key player in the supervised experience. It is interesting to note that much of the literature focuses on the administrative expectations of students in internships. These include meeting certain grade point requirements, completing course prerequisites, enrolling for a limited number of practicum units, and completing the appropriate paperwork (Schmidt et al., 1992). Others have described the steps students should take to ensure they receive any entitlements that might be associated with the experience. For example, Green (1997) suggests that students ask departments for a list of approved sites, verify the type of credit they will receive, inquire about transportation to and from the site, and ask whether they will be paid for their work or reimbursed for the expenses they will incur during the experience. Authors of this literature also describe how students should behave once they start working at the site, which includes asking questions, repeating instructions to ensure they are clear, being pleasant to coworkers, and adhering to the established work schedule (Green, 1997). Some have gone so far as to suggest that if the experience is not a positive one, that may be the fault of an "inappropriate student" who does not understand the complexity of an organizational setting (Alexander, 1982, p. 130).

From the perspective of this book, the student's role in the supervised experience goes beyond merely meeting administrative or behavioral requirements. Students need to be realistic in their expectations. They bring certain strengths and skills to the setting, including their interest in the work conducted at the site, their enthusiasm for that work, and their interest in the particular projects they will work on during the experience. Moreover, they bring a fresh perspective to the setting, seeing things others who have worked in that setting for longer periods of time may have overlooked. But students should also be prepared to deal with issues they did not expect when they contracted to work at the site.

Every organizational setting experiences periods of time when the work is more reactive than proactive, when tasks are highly routinized rather than highly challenging, when compliance is more appropriate than creativity.

Organizations are also political entities, and infighting is apparent at times, causing tension among coworkers and between units. Students should expect to encounter such issues during the course of the experience. Perhaps the most important thing they can remember is that they are there to learn about the organization and how it functions in the broadest sense. That learning includes developing an appreciation for the glamorous as well as the not-so-attractive underbelly of the setting. If students come away from a supervised experience with a thorough understanding of the organization and its inner workings, they can be more realistic about what to expect should they end up working in that, or a similar, setting. This kind of learning can be invaluable when identifying realistic professional aspirations.

The second key player in the supervised experience is the site supervisor, the person with whom the student will have the most contact over the course of the academic term. Authors who have written about the role of the supervisor, to some degree, parallel what has been written about the student role. Supervisors are directed to ensure that certain administrative functions occur, such as orienting the student to the functions of the office and documenting the time spent on the experience (Fender & Watson, 2005). In other cases, the behaviors supervisors are expected to exhibit are identified, including meeting regularly with students, training them on specific tasks, and integrating them into the setting (Dye & Bender, 2006; Mason, 1985). But some scholars take a more enlightened approach to the role of the supervisor. They encourage supervisors to realize that they play a dual role when working with students: supervisor and educator. As educators, supervisors need to recognize the stages that are associated with internships. These stages include exhilaration, rejection, integration, and transformation on the part of the student. If supervisors recognize the attributes associated with each stage, they can more effectively work with the student in a stage-relevant manner (Garvey & Vorsteg, 1992). In another sense, the supervisor serves as an interpreter, connecting the theory students have learned in the classroom with the work that is conducted in the real world (Sherman & Crum, 2009). (Readers are directed to Chapter 3 for a more complete discussion about the roles of the site supervisor and a developmental model of the internship experience.)

The final key player in the supervised experience is the faculty supervisor. Surprisingly, most of what has been written about faculty roles focuses on what they are not prepared to do. Many faculty members operate on the assumption that they are experts in their field. Their role in the classroom, therefore, is to impart that knowledge to students. They disdain the idea that they are responsible for job training. Fortunately, that is not usually the case in student affairs because it is an applied field, and most faculty members in this area have had experience as practitioners before becoming full-time faculty members. Faculty members, however, may not be current on the most recent developments in a functional area or the latest thinking about how to be responsive to student wants and needs. (See Chapter 3 for a detailed discussion of the faculty supervisor's roles and responsibilities.)

The Pedagogical Structure

The pedagogical structure of the supervised experience refers to the form the class associated with the internship assumes. There are a number of approaches to the pedagogical component described in the literature. Toohey et al. (1996) offer a particularly insightful discussion of several models. The attendance model describes a minimalist approach in which the class serves primarily as a means of ensuring that students are working at their sites and completing their assigned tasks. Slightly more advanced is the work history model in which the class is designed to demonstrate to students how they can capitalize on the tasks they are completing on site when they conduct a job search. The work history model is grounded in the assumption that since supervised practice experiences vary so much from student to student, there can be no coherent or structured learning experience for all internship students in a given term, so the class focuses on individual accomplishments. A more modified approach is the broad abilities model in which the faculty member identifies broad objectives for the learning component of the internship experience, including things such as critical thinking and the development of interpersonal skills. These abilities form the focus of the educational program, and the instructor strives to ensure that all students make gains in at least some of these abilities. The specific competencies model is a somewhat more structured approach to learning in which the faculty member identifies key competencies that all practicum students should learn on their sites and works to ensure that all students acquire these competencies. The advantages to such an approach relate to the consistency of performance it can ensure for students; the disadvantages relate to the degree of organization it takes to ensure that consistency.

The final model described in the Toohey et al. (1996) framework, the negotiated curriculum model, reflects the model most frequently used for supervised experiences in higher education and student affairs administration. In this model, the student, site supervisor, and faculty supervisor develop a contract that identifies the tasks the student will assume and the knowledge, skills, and competencies the student will gain from accomplishing those tasks. The advantages to this model include the higher levels of commitment and motivation students demonstrate when they are working on individualized agendas. The disadvantages relate to the enormous amount of effort it can take for the faculty member to individually negotiate each contract each academic term for each student.

We advocate a modified version of the negotiated curriculum model for faculty who teach the supervised experience class. Clearly, we believe that an individually designed contract is the most beneficial approach for the student and is likely the most beneficial approach for the organization in which the student works since the approach identifies specific tasks and responsibilities the intern will assume. But we suggest that the role of the faculty supervisor should extend beyond simply tracking the progress students make on their contracts over the course of the academic term.

Identifying the Resources Necessary to Conduct the Experience

Although the previous sections in this chapter have focused on the development of supervised practice experiences, there are two other issues students need to consider when they undertake such experiences. The first of these relates to the resources students may need to successfully complete the experience. The breadth and variety of the supervised experiences designed by students in higher education and student affairs programs makes it difficult to identify all the resources students may need, but we encourage students to consider their needs in four distinct areas when evaluating potential internship sites: personnel, facilities, equipment, and financial support. Figure 2.1 summarizes these resources.

```
                Resources Checklist

Personnel Resources
        Site Supervisor
        Faculty Supervisor
        Support Staff
        Other:
Facilities
        Workspace On-Site
        Meeting Rooms
        Classrooms
        Lab Access
        Approval to Work at Home
        Other:
Equipment
        Desk
        Filing Cabinet
        Phone
        Mailbox
        Copier Access
        FAX Access
        Office Supplies
        Computer
        Special Equipment
        Other:
Financial
        Salary/Stipend/Honorarium
        Travel to Site
        Project Travel
        Hidden Costs
        Insurance
        Other:
```

Figure 2.1 Resources checklist.

Personnel

The first of these resources, personnel, refers to the types of access students will have to the personnel who will play key roles in the supervised experience. Perhaps the most important resource in this area is the site supervisor. It is important that students negotiate the frequency and degree of access they will have to their site supervisor. Even though students may feel they need to confer with the supervisor frequently, they also need to recognize that most site supervisors are managing other personnel at the same time they are supervising the intern. A site supervisor's availability may be limited, a problem that is further exacerbated by the fact that the student is typically only in the office on certain days and during certain hours. Students should also recognize that the need to meet with the supervisor might vary during the course of the academic term. In some cases, frequent contact early in the assignment is necessary. In other cases, where students are working on long-term projects for example, the need to confer with the supervisor may arise later in the term. We encourage students to discuss in detail the time they will have with their site supervisor when designing the contract and include that time in the contract so that all parties are clear about the expectations.

Access to the faculty supervisor is the second form of support students need to consider when designing experiences. Even though students may be assured of some access to the faculty supervisor, both students and faculty members have other obligations they will be meeting during the academic term. For students who have internships at institutions far removed from the home campus (especially during the summer), face-to-face contact may be difficult, if not impossible. During the regular academic year, students may have other classes to attend and jobs or GA responsibilities to fulfill. Faculty are teaching other classes and working on other projects, but faculty supervisors are valuable resources for students in supervised experiences. These faculty members can assist students in resolving difficulties they encounter on the job and serve as sounding boards for students' ideas.

The third group of individuals who can serve as a resource for student interns is the support staff at the site, including receptionists, secretaries, accounting technicians, and others. These staff members are frequently overlooked when students and site supervisors design contracts. Although interns may provide valuable services to the units in which they work, they can also create an additional workload for support staff. Receptionists may be expected to take phone messages or schedule meetings for the intern. Secretaries may be expected to type materials or maintain files for the student. Accounting technicians may be expected to manage funding requests or manage budgets associated with the intern's work. If this is the case, support staff members ought to be advised of these expectations. Support staff can serve as powerful allies to students in supervised experiences. They can socialize the intern about the routines and procedures the office employs. They can make a big difference in how quickly the student becomes acclimated to the culture of the office. The services they provide are frequently overlooked or underrated. We urge students and site supervisors to recognize the important contributions these staff members can provide over the course of the supervised experience. (See Chapter 3 for additional discussion about working with support staff and potential pitfalls to avoid.)

Facilities

Another resource issue students and site and faculty supervisors need to address when designing experiences relates to facilities. Facilities include the space the student will need to conduct the work at the site and, at times, the facilities interns may need elsewhere on campus to complete their assigned responsibilities. Space on most college and university campuses is at a premium. In many cases, departments barely have sufficient space to accommodate their full-time employees, so finding space to house a graduate student intern can be difficult. However, if the experience is supposed to expose the student to the functioning of the department or office, having a designated workspace in the department or office setting is a necessity. At times, this may mean assigning the intern space in an office already occupied by other staff or GAs. Although sharing an office may not be ideal, it assures the intern of a place in the office in which work related to the experience can be conducted. When interns are assigned to shared space, we encourage them to work out suitable arrangements with their officemates and respect the roles that others in the space need to play. Interns also need to remember that to some degree they will always be viewed as visitors by those who work there regularly.

It is also important to consider other facilities that student interns may need to successfully meet the terms of their contracts. These may include meeting rooms, conference rooms, classrooms, or access to media or other labs on campus. The kinds of facilities that may be needed are directly related to the tasks the student has described in the contract. When additional facilities are needed, the supervisor may need to make arrangements with those who manage the facilities to provide access to the student. Alternatively, they may need to ensure that the intern is listed as an authorized staff member of the department so that she or he can reserve space as needed.

Finally, there may be some occasions or circumstances in which interns can conduct work related to the contract at home. Writing reports, making phone calls, or designing programs are activities that interns can conceivably conduct from their home settings. In fact, some students prefer to handle these kinds of assignments from home, particularly if they are sharing office space at the work site. Other students, however, prefer to distinguish their home environment from their work environment and may not be comfortable managing work tasks in the home setting. Each case is unique. But if students plan to conduct some of their assignments from home, they need to discuss this option with the site supervisor prior to finalizing the contract. It is important to remember, though, that the intern needs to spend a considerable amount of time in the work setting to observe and understand the intricate workings of the setting.

Equipment

Another resource that is frequently omitted in the process of planning supervised experiences is equipment. Again, the needs for equipment are directly related to the tasks defined in the contract. This makes it difficult to identify all the types of equipment that may be needed for the varied projects students assume in supervised experiences, but some items come immediately to mind. Interns need to know if they will have a desk, a filing cabinet, a telephone, a mailbox, access to a copier, access to a fax machine, use of a computer, or access to other equipment that they may need to fulfill their responsibilities. Even minor pieces of equipment such as work trays, index card holders, message boxes, staplers, or tape dispensers can be essential tools for students, depending on the nature of their assignments.

Related to office equipment is the issue of office supplies. Access to paper, message pads, pens, stencils, paper clips, and the like can affect the student's ability to complete assignments. Even though these may seem like minor matters, supplies are costly, particularly for units that are operating on limited budgets. A discussion about what kind of support the student can expect to receive with respect to office supplies can help avoid any problems or shortages that might arise after the intern starts working. It is particularly important that the site supervisor inform the support staff member who has responsibility for ordering and issuing office supplies about which kinds of intern requests should be honored and which require supervisor approval.

A desktop computer is a staple in most college and university offices. But providing the student with a computer also involves ensuring the student has the appropriate ancillary equipment (e.g., keyboard, printer access, monitor) as well as the appropriate software to operate that equipment and the specialized software that may be necessary to complete the projects designated in the contract. There also may be other forms of specialized equipment that interns will need. These may include audiotaping equipment, videotaping equipment, slide projectors, overhead projectors, LCDs, microphones, movie projectors and screens, or DVDs, among others. If there are costs associated with purchasing or renting that equipment, clear expectations about which party will incur those costs should be established.

Financial

The basic final resource students should consider when designing supervised experiences may be the most obvious: financial support. Like other resources, financial support needs to be linked to the activities that students are expected to engage in under the terms of the contract. The first that comes to mind is any form of pay the student might receive in conjunction with the work, including hourly wages, stipends, or honoraria. In most cases, there are institutional or departmental policies that dictate whether students are even eligible for such payments. Institutional policy may dictate whether interns are eligible to receive compensation. If interns are also enrolled students at the institution, they may not be eligible for stipends. Internships conducted at colleges or universities other than the intern's home institution, however, often qualify for remuneration. Some internships, typically those sponsored during the summer by professional associations such as Association of College and University Housing Officers-International (ACUHO-I), National Orientation Directors Association (NODA), and ACPA College Student Educators International, for instance, carry stipends and sometimes include housing and meals.

There are, however, other costs that may be incurred in connection with an internship. For example, students may need to travel to and from the site if the experience is not conducted at the home campus. Gas, mileage, and parking costs associated with such travel should be calculated into the expenses the student anticipates. Other forms of travel may be required to complete the projects identified in the contract. In some cases, travel to conferences, including registration fees, hotel and meal costs, and travel expenses may be incurred. Some site supervisors may offer to cover these expenses, or split the costs with the student, but there is no standard practice in this area. Again, it is imperative that students understand the potential costs associated with the projects they plan to undertake in their supervised experiences.

Finally, there may be other, hidden costs that students should consider when planning internships. In many cases, working in a professional capacity in an office will require appropriate dress. Many graduate students may not have wardrobes that meet the dress standards of the office. Accessories, including jackets, dress shoes, and briefcases might also be necessary. Depending on the nature of the contract, liability or some other form of insurance may be warranted. Many institutions require students in a supervised practice experience to have professional liability insurance, which may be obtained at relatively low cost by student members of NASPA and ACPA. Even if not required, interns are strongly advised to secure professional liability insurance before beginning the internship experience. Even though most campuses have policies in place to cover employees, students are urged to find out whether they, in their volunteer capacities, will be covered by such policies. Other expenses such as long-distance telephone calls made from home may be incurred. All these issues should be contemplated when designing contracts and discussed with the site supervisor.

Resources are important considerations in the supervised experience, considerations that are frequently overlooked by students and site supervisors. The resources that are available to interns and the costs associated with conducting the projects identified in the contract are concerns that should be addressed in the design stage of the process. We strongly encourage students and site supervisors to spend some time identifying all the resources that may be associated with each proposed project and to determine who will bear the responsibility for providing those resources. Such conversations can prevent misunderstandings between students and supervisors once the student has started working on site.

Reflection Activity

1. For one week, keep a list of the resources you use in your current assistantship or job. At the end of the week, sort the resources into personnel, facilities, equipment, and financial resources.
2. Use this list to identify the resources you might need in an internship.
3. Identify people you can turn to for advice about resources.

Balancing the Experience With Other Curriculum Components and Student Lives

The final component that needs to be addressed in any discussion of supervised experiences relates to the overall management of the experience. By overall management, we mean the balance that students need to achieve within the context of the experience itself as well as between the experience and the other responsibilities in their lives. The individualized nature of the supervised experience, and the concomitant motivation that usually accompanies that experience, can disrupt the normal sense of balance. To this end, students may need to address many of the following issues in relation to the internship.

On-Site Balance

The first group of concerns relates to maintaining a balance within the context of the supervised practice setting. The most obvious of these is the balance that students need to maintain among the various projects they agree to complete as part of the contract. It is not unusual for students to identify projects at the outset that they find are not particularly interesting or challenging once they actually start working on them. In other instances, students may identify some projects that get much more complex than they first anticipated. A tempting response to either of these scenarios is to simply ignore that particular task or project and devote more time to the other components of the contract. This is seldom a judicious path to take. The purpose of the supervised experience is to provide students with opportunities to learn. Learning does not occur when students avoid certain components of their contracts. Interns should also remember that evaluation of the intern and awarding of course grades are based in to a substantial degree on fulfilling the internship contract. Students who encounter challenges in balancing projects should discuss their concerns with their site supervisors. Supervisors may be able to provide some guidance that will enable the student to regain a balance among assignments. It may be that revisions in the contract are warranted. In either case, the resolution ought to be negotiated with the site supervisor as soon as difficulties arise. To raise the issue in the last week of the internship may not lead to a satisfactory resolution of any problems.

The second form of balance students need to maintain within the internship context is the issue of dependence versus independence. By this we mean the degree to which students feel free to act on their own versus the times when they feel obligated to seek close supervision. There is no easy formula to guide students in this endeavor. We can only suggest that there are times when greater dependence may be warranted. For example, many interns need extra guidance when they first start working at the site or when they undertake a new project. As more time is spent on site, it is likely that students will feel more comfortable acting independently or with more limited guidance. We encourage students to ask their supervisors if they are acting appropriately under different circumstances. Particularly early in the internship, interns should request general guidelines from the site supervisor about her or his expectations in this regard. (See Chapter 3 for the discussion of the developmental process in the intern–site supervisor relationship.)

The final issue to be addressed in the context of the internship setting is the balance between training and learning. We have argued here and elsewhere in this book that the supervised practice experience is an important component of the graduate education curriculum. It is relatively easy, however, for both students and site supervisors to focus more on the training element of the experience and less on the educational element. After all, the student is expected to behave as a professional, and supervisors are encouraged to treat the student as they would any other inexperienced professional. These expectations readily lead to treating the supervised experience as a job-training experience. From the perspective of this book, an internship should be much more. Even though on-the-job training is certainly a component of the internship experience, it is only one component of that experience. If students or supervisors realize that they have not talked about what the student has learned or have not discussed the relationship between what the student has learned in classes and what the student has learned on the job, it may be time to revisit the issue of balance between training and learning.

Balance Between the Internship and Other Responsibilities

There are also issues of balance between the supervised experience and the other responsibilities students have in any given academic term. The most obvious of these is the balance between the supervised experience and the other classes that the student may be taking. Supervised practice experiences are often taken in the middle or toward the end of the student's program of study after sufficient classroom learning has occurred to prepare the student for the experience. As the student nears completion of the degree, the issue of finding a job becomes more important. It is easy to rationalize that devoting more time and energy to the internship will better serve the student in the job-search process. Focusing extensively on the supervised experience, however, diminishes the time and energy the student can devote to other classes. Because completing all courses is required to earn the degree, students need to keep the benefits of the experience in perspective. Finding the proper balance between the internship and other classes enables the student to achieve both the degree and the opportunity to pursue the position of their dreams.

Most students in internships also have responsibilities outside of coursework. Many serve as GAs or hold jobs outside the campus. Again, it is incumbent upon students to remember *all* their obligations, both the internship site and the outside employer. It is important to remember that their supervisors at those other jobs are likely to serve as references when the student searches for a professional position. It is likely that GA or job supervisors have employed the student for a longer period than the internship supervisor. Students need to balance the demands of their competing jobs to ensure that they adequately meet all their responsibilities.

Finally, many of the most frequently ignored responsibilities students in higher education or student affairs graduate programs encounter are personal in nature. Many students have spouses, partners, children, or other family members for whom they provide care. Nurturing such relationships requires time and energy. The basic philosophy that guides student affairs is the holistic development of the student. This involves promoting their development intellectually, socially, emotionally, physically, spiritually, and personally. Unfortunately many successful professionals do not model a well-rounded lifestyle. They work well more than 40 hours per week and often devote evenings and weekends to job-related activities. Graduate students may be particularly prone to focusing too much on their studies and campus jobs at the expense of their personal responsibilities or find themselves in time squeezes due to dysfunctional time management skills, poor planning, or inadequate impulse control. Finding a balance between the expectations of the internship and other academic demands and personal demands is not easy. We would argue, however, that students who try to balance their lives while in graduate school will be much better prepared to balance those competing demands once they finish their degrees and assume full-time positions.

Conclusion

In conclusion, the internship can be nothing more than on-the-job training, or it can be one of the most meaningful learning experiences in the student's curriculum. The success of the experience depends to a large extent on how purposefully it is designed. A successful experience is one that is intentional in its design. Intentional designs are grounded in careful assessments of skills and selective designations of objectives. These objectives should be translated into a carefully crafted contract that clearly delineates what the student will do and what skills and competencies the student should work on developing. Other issues such as the resources needed to complete the terms of the contract should also be addressed before work at the site begins. Finally, it is essential to keep the supervised experience in perspective and to balance the time and energy devoted to the experience with the other responsibilities of the student. If all these components are addressed when designing the supervised experience, students can maximize the benefits of the experience and accrue all of the important learning that can occur through the supervised experience.

References

Alexander, J. R. (1982). Institutional design of public service internships: Conceptual, academic, and structural problems. *Teaching Political Science, 9,* 127–133.

American College Personnel Association (ACPA)/National Association of Student Affairs Administrators (NASPA). (2010). *Professional competency areas for student affairs practitioners.* Washington, DC: American College Personnel Association and National Association of Student Personnel Administrators.

Beenen, G., & Rousseau, D. M. (2010), Getting the most from MBA internships: Promoting intern learning and job acceptance. *Human Resource Management, 49,* 3–22. doi:10.1002/hrm.20331

Carter, R., Cooke, F., & Neal, B. (1996). Action-centered learning in industry. In J. Tait & P. Knight (Eds.), *The management of independent learning* (pp. 65–73). London: Koga Page.

Ciofalo, A. (1992). What every professor and work-site supervisor should know about internships. In A. Ciofalo (Ed.), *Internships: Perspectives on experiential learning* (pp. 52–73). Malabar, FL: Krieger.

Delve, C. I., Mintz, S. D., & Stewart, G. M. (Eds.). (1990). *Community service as values education.* New Directions for Student Services, No. 50. San Francisco, CA: Jossey-Bass.

Dye, D. C., & Bender, D. (2006). Duty and liability surrounding clinical internships: What every internship coordinator should know. *Journal of Allied Health, 35*(3), 169–173.

Featherman, S. (1998). Higher education in the United States: Changing markets and evolving values. In S. M. Natale, R. P. Hoffman, & G. Hayward (Eds.), *Business education and training: A value-laden process: Volume V: The Management of values: Organizational and educational issues* (pp. 25–33). New York, NY: University Press of America.

Fender, D. L., & Watson L. E. (2005). OSH Internships: One program's perspective on benefits for students, employers and universities. *Professional Safety, 50*(4), 36–40. Retrieved from ABI/INFORM Global (Document ID: 820628171).

Garvey, D., & Vorsteg, A. C. (1992). From theory to practice for college interns: A stage theory approach. *Journal of Experiential Education, 15*(2), 40–43.

Green, M. W. (1997). *Internship success: Real-world, step-by-step advice on getting the most out of internships.* Chicago, IL: VGM Career Horizons.

Mason, G. E. (1985, April). *Coordinating the internship program: The ins and outs of directing interns.* Paper presented at the annual conference of the Central States Speech Association, Indianapolis, IN.

McCormick, D. W. (1993). Critical thinking, experiential learning, and internships. *Journal of Management Education, 17,* 260–262.

Miller, T. K. (Ed.). (2001). *The CAS book of professional standards for higher education.* Washington, DC: Council for the Advancement of Standards in Higher Education.

Murphy, S., & Kaffenberger, C. (2007). ASCA national model®: The foundation for supervision of practicum and internship students. *Professional School Counseling, 10*(3), 289–296.

Narayanan, V. K., Olk, P. M., & Fukami, C. V. (2010). Determinants of internship effectiveness: An exploratory model. *Academy of Management Learning and Education, 9*(1), 61–80.

Ryan, M., & Cassidy, J. R. (1996). Internships and excellence. *Liberal Education, 82*(3), 16–23.

Saunders, S. A., & Cooper, D. L. (2001). Programmatic interventions: Translating theory to practice. In R. B. Winston, Jr., D. G. Creamer, T. K. Miller, & Associates, *The professional student affairs administrator: Educator, leader, and manager.* New York, NY: Brunner-Routledge.

Schmidt, W. V., Gardner, G. H., Benjamin, J. B., Conaway, R. N., & Haskins, W. A. (1992, October). *Teaching the college course series: Directing independent studies and internships in communication.* Paper presented at the annual meeting of the Speech Communication Association, Chicago, IL.

Sherman, W. H., & Crum, K. S. (2009). Designing the internship in educational leadership as a transformative tool for improved practice. *International Journal of Educational Reform, 18*(1), 63–81.

Stewart, G. M. (1994). *Skills analysis survey for graduate students in higher education and student affairs graduate preparation programs.* Unpublished manuscript, University of Maryland at College Park.

Taylor, M. S. (1992). Effects of college internships on individual participants. In A. Ciofalo (Ed.), *Internships: Perspectives on experiential learning* (pp. 52–73). Malabar, FL: Krieger.

Toohey, S., Ryan, G., & Hughes, C. (1996). Assessing the practicum. *Assessment and Evaluation in Higher Education, 21,* 215–227.

Winston, R. B., Jr., Lathrop, B. J., Lease, J., Davis, J. S., Newsome, K., & Beeny, C. (2001). *Supervised practice in student affairs preparation: State of the art.* Unpublished manuscript, University of Georgia.

Part Two

3 Supervision and Other Relationships That Support Learning

Optimal learning from a practical experience, such as a practicum, assistant-ship, internship, or volunteer opportunity, is dependent on two factors. First is the quality of relationships a student can establish with the supervisor, colleagues, and clientele of the office. The best relationships are those that foster high expectations for interns' performance balanced by support for their questions and guidance for problem solving. Second, the learning from supervised practice is dependent on the willingness of the intern to take initiative, even in ambiguous real-life situations, and to seek advice, perspective about the culture, and candid feedback from others in the office. Building these relationships is essentially a two-way street in which interns bear a great deal of responsibility for the learning that evolves.

In this chapter, we will explain the nature of the supervision relationship as well as strategies an intern can use to gain the most benefit from all the relationships available in a supervised practice site. Further, we will discuss ways to avoid or cope with common problems that may occur in the site.

Understanding the Context

The supervised practice experience is more than simply *doing, observing, or working*. The overriding purpose for the experience is learning by the intern. For learning to be maximized, interns must observe; read and collect information; perform professional-level tasks; reflect on what they have seen; and receive frequent candid feedback about performance, demeanor, and attitudes. Consequently, supervision is a crucial component in the successful supervised practice experience.

To fully understand the elements of supervision, one needs to recognize the culture of the institution, realities of the setting, and multiple roles performed by supervisors. Without this understanding it is easy to create unrealistic expectations of the supervisory relationship and the potential contributions of other staff and clientele.

The supervised practice experience is a vital part of the total professional preparation program, but it varies from classroom-based courses in several important ways. Because these sites are in the *real world*, they are often different, in both positive and negative ways, from descriptions provided in textbooks and professional journals. Several aspects of supervised practice sites need to be recognized.

Supervised practice relationships occur within the context of an organizational culture. To be successful, interns must quickly discern the often-unstated elements of an organization's culture. A particular office staff has its own way of doing things, determining what initiatives have value, and interacting with each other. Chapter 6 contains detailed information about the ways in which institutional type and organizational culture shape an internship. Supervisors can and should be interpreters of organizational culture—explaining the reasoning and context of office behavior and expectations (Tull, Hirt, & Saunders, 2009). In many cases, however, the intern needs to request these types of explanations from the supervisor.

Further, the organizational culture shapes the nature of the supervisory relationship. In certain office cultures, for example, supervision is a shared activity where many staff members offer feedback directly to the intern. In other offices it is considered appropriate for only the designated supervisor to communicate comments on intern performance.

Reflection Activity

If possible, have a conversation with your site supervisor or another professional in your setting discussing how he or she learned the institutional and organizational culture. What are some ways that you can adapt those strategies for yourself?

Primary mission of supervised practice sites. Supervised practice sites are not created to train interns, unlike classroom-based instruction, which is designed solely for the purpose of educating enrolled students. Supervised practice sites exist to fulfill institutional responsibilities. As a consequence, should there be a conflict between the needs of preparation program students and fulfilling the site's primary mission, the intern's needs invariably and appropriately must be given a lower priority. Interns should be thoroughly aware of the primary mission of the chosen site and be flexible in their expectations of how the site can serve their needs.

Site supervisors and other supporters as working professionals. From the perspective of professional preparation, site supervisors generally are volunteers who agree to accept preparation program students and to provide supervision as a responsibility above and beyond their customary work assignments. In many offices, a number of professional staff members—other than the designated site supervisor—assist, guide, and teach graduate interns. Except in rare instances, site supervisors or others receive no additional monetary compensation for the work they do in their supervised practice roles. In addition, because supervising preparation program students is often not a major part of staff members' *official* job descriptions, they may not receive adequate recognition from their administrative unit's leadership. Site supervisors and others usually serve these functions because of a sense of professional responsibility and out of a desire to make a contribution to professional preparation. Realistically, students also must understand that there may be considerable variability in the level of commitment that site supervisors and others can provide over the course of the experience because other responsibilities might be more pressing.

Reflection Activity

1. As a way to learn about your setting and the multiple obligations of colleagues in your site, obtain a copy of the organizational chart. Determine who reports to whom and how your unit connects to others at the college or university. Focus particular attention on your site supervisor and answer the following questions:
    a.   How many other staff members does he or she manage?
    b.   What are the particular functions for which he or she has responsibility?
2. Look carefully at your unit's website and address the following questions:
    a.   What activities or functions do your colleagues and supervisor manage?
    b.   Based on the website information, what would you anticipate to be particularly busy times for your office or particularly stressful or demanding events?

Dealing with the unanticipated. One of the hallmarks of work in student affairs is the variety of issues, problems, and concerns that one is called on to address daily. In settings that deal with students' out-of-class life, work in student affairs is seldom routine and cannot be completely anticipated from day to day (even hour to hour on some days). Because of the unpredictability of the challenges staff members face in their customary duties, sometimes the best plans for supervision must be changed on short notice. Flexibility is a needed attribute for interns engaged in a supervised practice experience.

Levels of supervisor expertise and experience. Seldom do site supervisors have extensive training in supervising staff or interns. In a recent national study

(Gutierrez et al., 2010), only about 60% of the middle-level managers surveyed received training in supervising staff. According to Winston and Creamer (1997), an even smaller number of practitioners have received instruction in supervising student interns. Consequently, most site supervisors are learning as they go or have developed their style and techniques through observation of others or trial and error. Given this situation, interns need to adjust to supervisors' multiple responsibilities and supervision style and be explicit about their needs and desires. Discerning interns help their supervisors by telling them what they feel they need; sending subtle messages may not be sufficient. On the other hand, interns must be cognizant of the supervised practice limitations: what an intern wants or needs may not be realistic in a given setting or may require more than a site supervisor is able or willing to provide.

Further, interns may work with site supervisors who have had their own training in disciplines that are different from higher education and student affairs administration. These supervisors may not share the same knowledge base as the intern, and they may not use the same conceptual frameworks to guide their practice. However, the opportunity to work with supervisors and others whose expertise is in business affairs or a liberal arts or technical discipline, for example, can be especially rewarding because the intern is exposed to expectations and worldviews quite different from what is typical among student affairs professionals.

In the end, interns have influence over the quality of supervision and working relationships in their setting. It is important to remember that receiving quality guidance in the workplace is a two-way responsibility. Discovering colleagues' professional values, academic background, and areas of professional interest is an important part of developing quality relationships that support learning.

Reflection Activity

1. Search the office website for biographies of your supervisor and other colleagues. You might need to search other sources or ask your colleagues directly for information about their backgrounds.

2. Address the following questions:
   a. What type of academic backgrounds do your colleagues have?
   b. What are their particular professional interests? You might be able to determine this from professional association involvements, publications, presentations, or committee appointments on campus.
   c. What are your educated guesses about the values and priorities of your supervisor and colleagues based on their backgrounds?
   d. How might you determine the validity of these educated guesses?

Variability among sites. Supervised practice sites deal with real people who have real problems and issues, in an institution that has a history of both success and failure, and in a constantly changing society. As a consequence, when interns look below the surface, they see that most supervised practice sites have shortcomings and imperfections as well as hidden excellence. Some sites are doing sophisticated, innovative work and are leaders in their functional area. Other sites are solid; they are not doing much that can be classified as new or highly innovative, but students evaluate their programs positively, and the sites are considered in the mainstream of their functional areas. Some sites may be less developed due to a variety of reasons, including a lack of institutional support, new leadership, uncertainty of mission, lack of staff, or other circumstances.

Sites may also have different approaches to structuring the supervised practice opportunity. For example, certain sites have developed well-articulated plans for supervision and structuring the work, with clearly defined procedures, policy manuals, and accountability measures. Other sites may lack a highly structured approach where the intern will be exposed to greater ambiguity. On most campuses, sites also vary in their degree of experience in working with interns engaged in supervised practice. Valuable learning can be acquired in any of the types of settings just described. In many instances, interns learn more significant lessons and skills in settings that require more effort on their part than in more well-established and structured environments.

Reflection Activity

1. How would you describe your site in terms of its approach to supervised practice?
   a. Is it highly structured or more flexible?
   b. What are other characteristics of your site's approach to supervised practice?
   c. In what ways might these approaches be comfortable or challenging for your own professional growth?
2. What are some of the hidden learning opportunities in your site? How might you work with your supervisor or others in your site to structure these opportunities? Be as specific as possible in outlining next steps to make the most of these learning opportunities.

Thus, the realities of supervised practice settings call upon interns to be cognizant of characteristics, both subtle and overt, of the setting and the actual types of experiences available to them. Not only must interns be astute observers of the site and staff, but they must also articulate what they need, what they can contribute, and how they learn.

Supervision: Definition and Purpose

For the purposes of this book, supervision is a method of training and teaching in which experienced professionals provide guidance, opportunities for skill development, crucial feedback, and general support in a field setting to interns who are enrolled in a professional preparation program. It is an interactive, collaborative process in which both the supervisor and intern make vital contributions. Ideally, it is a synergetic process in that the total effect of the supervision process is greater than the sum of individual contributions. (See Winston & Creamer [1997] for a complete discussion of this process in professional staff supervision.) High-quality supervision is essential if interns are to have an optimal learning experience. Usually, the quality of supervision is a central determinant of the educational value of the supervised practice and is far more important than opulent facilities, large unit budgets, a large number of staff members, or size and type of institution.

In some circumstances, the intern receives supervision from two sources: the site supervisor and the faculty supervisor. Both site and faculty supervisors play multiple, complementary roles. In the sections to follow, we discuss the purposes that site supervision plays in the supervised practice experience and present a model of developmental stages through which many intern–supervisor relationships progress. Following that, we address the faculty supervisor's roles and functions.

Site Supervision

Good site supervision is based on (a) a trusting and supportive relationship between supervisor and intern, (b) an organizational structure that permits interns to observe widely and to assume some responsibilities normally associated with professionals in the site, (c) articulation of the theory and conceptual frameworks that undergird practice, (d) open communication and candor, (e) mutual respect, (f) practice that emphasizes observance of professional ethical standards, and (g) ongoing evaluation of performance.

The effective site supervision relationship has several distinctive characteristics. The relationship is unequal in terms of power, status, and expertise. Therefore, although the interactions can be cordial and mutually respectful, one must maintain boundaries to avoid confusing friendship with supervision and to permit candid evaluations and feedback. It is important to remember that fundamentally a supervisory relationship exists to fulfill a two fold purpose: to promote the intern's learning and to fulfill the responsibilities of the office. Supervisors may become long-term mentors who promote career development for many years after graduate school, but these more intense mentoring relationships are not necessary for effective supervision to occur.

Important learning opportunities occur with site supervisors who can help the intern articulate the connections between the concepts and research findings they have been discussing in class and actual practice. Although interns can and should reflect independently on these connections, guidance from a site supervisor will likely provide richer insights. Also, some site supervisors may use theories or conceptual frameworks that are not covered in the graduate program curriculum. In these circumstances, it is important for the intern to learn the theories used at the site. A good strategy is to read research articles or texts that explain the conceptual frameworks and then to discuss the readings with the site supervisor.

Open communication between supervisors and supervisees makes the student's learning easier and less frustrating (Kiser, 2013). Ideally, interns should feel free to ask questions about anything pertinent to the learning experience without fear of causing conflict or being perceived as disrespectful. On the other hand, however, interns should construct their questions in ways that are diplomatic and that do not diminish the work of the site.

Supervised practices are more likely to flourish in ethical environments and languish in environments that do not adhere to principles of civility and fairness. In ethical environments, professional ethics are frequently discussed and explicitly influence actions. In these environments, interns are involved in discussions of ethical issues facing the unit and, consequently, are exposed to some of the most important questions that practitioners encounter. Sometimes interns may not question ethics for fear of being perceived to be questioning the professionalism of the site. If talking about ethics seems uncomfortable, interns should seek guidance from faculty or other trusted advisers.

Finally, supervisors and interns can maximize learning by establishing an evaluation process to monitor progress in both task completion and growth in professionalism. Chapter 4 contains strategies for structuring evaluations that should occur throughout the supervised practice, not just at the end of the experience. Regular and systematic evaluation is essential for learning and improvement. If an ongoing evaluation system is not apparent at the site, interns should request systematic feedback.

Roles of the Site Supervisor

Site supervisors play multiple roles in the life of the intern (Kiser, 2013). Foremost, site supervisors are *teachers*. In that role, they seek to create conditions that will allow the intern to (a) experience the full range of activities associated with the setting, (b) acquire necessary knowledge and information about the area, (c) gain insight into the formal and informal organizational functioning, (d) develop skills through hands-on experience functioning in a professional role, and (e) gain direct experience interacting with the office's clientele.

Site supervisors are *limit setters* who establish the parameters of the intern's work. Depending on the setting, there may be functions or records that are inappropriate, perhaps even illegal, for a graduate student to access. Additionally, some areas or functions of a site may require greater skill and knowledge than graduate students possess. There also may be some activities that are too politically or legally sensitive. It is the site supervisor's responsibility to protect interns from situations where the intern does not have the capacity to be successful, either because of expertise, position within the institution, or time available.

Supervisors are also *enablers* who create conditions within the unit that provide the student with introductions to staff, clientele, and other important players at the site. Supervisors define the student's role to others within the unit and make it possible for the student to make use of institutional resources, such as office space, telephones, office supplies, and computers.

Site supervisors are *models* of professionalism in the functional area. Through observation of supervisors and other staff in the setting, interns also can observe the use of expertise and experience to solve problems and accomplish the functional area's mission. On occasion supervisors and colleagues may inadvertently serve as negative role models; that is, interns may see leadership characteristics and ways of dealing with situations that are ineffective or counterproductive. Both positive and negative modeling are necessary for interns to experience as they form the visions of the kind of professionals they want to become.

Another site supervisor role is that of *sponsor*. Because of their experience and longevity in the field, supervisors can assist interns in meeting other practitioners within the institution and beyond and becoming acquainted with leaders in professional associations. Supervisors are well positioned to assist interns in the initial stages of building a professional network.

Site supervisors are also *evaluators* of learning, professional demeanor, and work performance. It is important for interns to remember that this important function of site supervisors requires them to give both positive and negative feedback about intern attitudes or behaviors that could be sensitive: how one is perceived by clientele or colleagues, how one communicates with different constituencies, or how one does or does not act in a professional or ethical manner. Chapter 4 outlines specific strategies for evaluation.

Getting the most from these site supervision functions requires that the student initiate open and candid communication from the beginning of the experience. The following Reflection Activity provides a structure for an early, candid conversation with the site supervisor.

Reflection Activity

Preparation: This activity should be completed within the first two weeks at your site—and earlier if possible. The purpose is to begin establishing a positive, open working relationship with supervisor and to clarify a variety of specific information necessary for effective supervised practice. The first step is to read through all of the questions and topics.

Then think through how you might approach a conversation with your site supervisor to address these items in a way that works in your particular context. You could modify questions, add topics to talk about, or delete some that don't seem to fit your situation.

You also should think through how you can best introduce this conversation to your supervisor. If possible, the conversation should be conducted in a private setting where both parties aren't rushed or pressured with other responsibilities.

Discussion Questions

1. How would you describe your learning preferences to your supervisor? (You may want to use the frameworks presented in Chapter 1 to structure your description.)
2. What does your supervisor think are the most valuable contributions they can make to your learning?
3. What can your site supervisor do (or refrain from doing) that will best facilitate your learning and productivity?
4. How does your supervisor describe her or his particular style of supervision?
5. How do you plan to build positive relationships with others in the setting? What guidance does your supervisor have about your plan?
6. What behaviors of students in supervised practice does your supervisor find most troublesome or aggravating?

Information to Cover

1. Nature of work (e.g., inquire about projects and special assignments).
2. Working conditions (e.g., determine desk space, use of telephone and computer).
3. Schedule of work. Make sure that the schedule is explicit and that the supervisor knows when you will be in the setting each week. Inform site supervisor well in advance if there are dates when you plan to be away from campus or have other commitments during regularly scheduled hours or days.
4. How and with whom you should communicate in case are unable to be in the setting when scheduled.
5. When to schedule supervision sessions. It is important that sessions occur weekly.
6. Dress (both in and out of the office) and behavior code for socializing with students, for example (when, where, and how), and means of address for site staff: Dr., Mr., Ms., first name?
7. Dates of special events in the unit and your anticipated involvement, if any.

8. Relationships with others in the unit (e.g., support, professional and paraprofessional staff, students).
9. Reporting lines. Find out to whom you report for what. In some settings, you may report to different people for differ projects or activities.
10. Readings and other information sources. Ask your supervisor to identify resources that can help you understand the functional area better.

Stages in the Development of the Supervisory Relationship

Most, although not all, successful relationships between interns and site supervisors go through identifiable developmental stages. It is not possible to present a highly prescriptive model because this relationship

> involves a unique combination of professional and life experiences, personal qualities, similarities, and differences. It requires an interweaving of teaching and learning styles and active communication on a regular basis. Each of the individuals involved brings strengths and weaknesses to the project of constructing a working relationship that will be of mutual benefit.
>
> (Chiaferi & Griffin, 1997, p. 25)

The developmental stage model presented in this chapter describes a successful, fully functioning supervisory relationship. In the real world of higher education, however, not all supervisory relationships will progress through all the stages. We believe that the model describes optimal functioning that is achieved in many supervised practices, although not all. Figure 3.1 offers an overview of the schema.

Induction stage. The first stage involves gaining entrée into the supervised practice setting. This includes learning one's way around, meeting professional and support staff, setting learning outcomes, negotiating the specifics of the supervised practice experience, and perhaps becoming acquainted with the geographic region if the supervised practice is in an area with which the intern is unfamiliar. At this stage, interns need to ask for structure (what to do, when, and how) and for emotional support as they face a great deal of new—people, tasks, structure—in a short period of time. If the site has a supervised practice handbook, much of the factual information can be placed where interns can consult it as the need arises. Most interns have a heightened level of anxiety and self-doubt that most people experience when entering a new situation.

Interns should be clear and specific about what they most want to learn as a result of the supervised practice experience. They should not expect the site supervisor to be a mind reader. Interns should not be hesitant to tell the supervisor when suggested or planned activities do not address supervised practice

Stages	Intern Needs	Tasks	Supervision Strategies
Induction Stage	• Entrée • Information • Structure • Emotional support • Exploration of role of novice	• To know and become known by others in site and in areas of usual interaction • To learn about the host institution and its mission, history, and aspirations • To learn about the internship site—its goals, procedures, history, and policies—as quickly as possible • To learn about the functional area in a general or generic sense (regionally and nationally) and in different types of institutions (e.g., community colleges, research universities, liberal arts colleges) • To establish supervisor expectations and have clear guidelines governing responsibilities, authority, and operating procedures • To feel at home • To feel competent	• Spend as much time as possible with intern and get to know on personal level • Introduce intern to staff, students, and others with whom he or she is likely to have interaction • Inform other staff about intern's assignments and lay ground rules for interactions • Clearly spell out expectations, written and unwritten rules of conduct, deadlines for completion of assignments or projects • Assist intern to operationalize internship learning outcomes • Establish a trusting, mutually respectful, warm, caring relationship
Acclimation Stage	• Increased self-awareness • Confidence in abilities • Feedback about attitudes and performance • Clarification about culture, history, and issues that affect practice	• To deal with dependency-autonomy conflicts • To take on limited professional roles • To take initiative • To be accountable • To become conversant with the literature of the functional area	• Begin to remove some structure • Offer praise for effective performance (look for things to commend) • Gently confront attitude problems and performance shortfalls • Share insights into the culture and teach intern how to read culture • Give intern assignments with clear responsibility and considerable autonomy
Application Stage	• Exploration of using theory in practice • Greater autonomy • Opportunity to apply knowledge and skills acquired in the classroom	• To analyze programs and services from theoretical perspectives • To complete complex assignment(s) • To solidify professional identity in the functional area	• Initiate discussion of theory use in specific activities • Assign intern project or task with near total autonomy • Move relationship more toward that of peer-to-peer or professional colleague • Confront shortcomings more assertively
Closure Stage	• Closure • Detailed feedback about performance • Fit learning from internship experience into career plans	• To integrate learning • To finish projects and assignments • To bring closure to relationships • To pass information and materials to the person who will assume the intern's responsibilities	• Treat intern as colleague • Provide opportunities to say good-bye • Provide thorough, behaviorally anchored evaluation • Assist intern in devising a professional development agenda

Figure 3.1 Developmental stages, needs, tasks, and strategies of the supervisory relationship.

learning goals. Interns should be prepared, however, to do some things that they may not particularly enjoy or find exciting because it is important that interns experience the full scope of work that goes on in the supervised practice site. Supervisors may insist that interns do certain things simply because it is a major responsibility of the functional area. Also, interns can expect to do a certain amount of work that is not intellectually challenging or personally rewarding (such as making copies, taking notes at meetings, or answering the telephone) simply because the tasks must be done and everyone in the setting is expected to pitch in. Early in the supervised practice experience interns may be called on to do more of what would be termed busy work simply because they are not yet knowledgeable enough about the site to work with students or to directly help site colleagues fulfill their duties.

At this stage, interns need to accomplish several tasks. It is important, for example, that interns become thoroughly familiar with the site and what others expect of it in the institution. Interns need to achieve cultural competence (Kuh, Siegel, & Thomas, 2001) to become fully aware of crucial nuances of the site. They may do this through careful and systematic assessment of the environment, including its people, technologies, goals, policies, procedures, and history. This assessment and this developing cultural competence can be accomplished simultaneously with establishing clear expectations between the site supervisor and the intern.

Supervisors must accomplish several crucial goals during this stage also. It is incumbent upon them, for example, to begin the investment of time with an intern that is essential to the type of relationship that will optimize learning. During this time, supervisors must ensure that others know interns in the office and all site personnel understand the purpose and goals for the internship. Groundwork should be laid to enable all within the site to contribute to the intern's learning experiences. Expectations of both the supervisor and the intern should be clear and explicit and should be established during this stage. The supervisor should show the intern the ways of accomplishing goals within the site (the ways of doing business in the office) and should promote an open, trusting, and mutually respectful relationship. When the proper grounds for learning oriented relationship have been established, the relationship can move to the next stage.

Acclimation stage. This stage evolves from the induction stage as the interns become more comfortable in the setting and begin to know their way around the site and institution. The intern is less dependent on the supervisor and other staff for direction or basic information. Self-confidence increases as interns experience success in completing assigned tasks and as they are given positive feedback for good work or constructive criticism for inadequate performance. Interns can assume greater responsibility and feel less of a need for continuous feedback and encouragement from the supervisor. Through conversation with staff and reading of the professional literature, interns become more adept at using the functional area's jargon. They begin to see themselves not as students but as professional practitioners, in at least some areas.

During this stage, interns take definitive steps toward accountability with the office. They take initiative toward becoming fully functioning professionals as they become familiar with the literature and other artifacts of the office, and they become more autonomous in their relationships.

Supervisors give interns more responsibility during this stage. Supervisors should have established a pattern of feedback that results in more professional behavior by the intern, and they allow more autonomy in organizing and carrying out duties and assignments. During this stage supervisors should instruct the intern in the cultural nuances of the office and the institution and generally help the intern feel more confident in her or his competencies.

Application stage. This stage might be called the optimal working stage and occurs when the intern is fully acclimated to the site, knows all the players and their personalities, understands something of the recent history of the site and the institution, and can see the site's strengths and weaknesses. The conversations between interns and supervisors become more philosophical and theoretical in nature; interns and supervisors can openly communicate without fear of offending and can analyze program successes and failures honestly—taking into account theory, institutional politics, personalities, and institutional culture. The relationship becomes truly collegial. The content of conversations is treated as confidential. Because the relationship is built on trust and mutual respect, supervisors can give interns sensitive frank feedback, accompanied with offers of assistance to correct difficulties. Interns are also empowered to give supervisors frank, critical feedback as well. The intern's needs are met through this process and the expected stage-related tasks become integrated into routines at the site.

Closure stage. The final stage of the relationship centers on closure. The content of supervisory sessions focus on terminating the intern–supervisor relationship, taking stock of what has been learned and what still needs to be learned, exploring the intern's career plans, and reflecting on where the internship experience fits into the overall preparation experience. Ideally, interns should leave the on-site experience with a professional development agenda they plan to pursue in the next few months or years. The final stage of the relationship also should focus on assisting the intern to integrate fully what has been learned during the experience into the intern's professional life.

Getting the Most From Your Site Supervisor

There are several things that graduate students can do to increase the probability that they will get the most possible from supervision in their setting.

Plan for Regular Supervision Sessions

At the beginning of the experience, a schedule of supervision sessions should be planned and placed on the supervisor's and intern's calendars. If the supervisor does not suggest this, the intern should request it, explaining that he or

she values face-to-face supervision and wants to make sure that there is sufficient time available.

Carefully Prepare for Supervision Sessions

Because time is valuable to both the supervisor and the intern, the content of
supervision sessions should be planned ahead of the session. Kiser (2013) suggests that interns prepare a meeting agenda that includes written summaries of
important events that need to be discussed and a list of questions and concerns.
It may also be important to gather data and information related to the questions and concerns and share those as well. Another helpful practice is for the
intern to send the agenda to the supervisor a few days in advance of the meeting. Ideally, the supervisor will also generate a list of discussion topics prior to
the meeting.

Request Frequent Feedback

If the supervisor does not volunteer it, interns should request feedback about
their progress in completing specific tasks or projects. Perhaps more importantly, interns should solicit feedback about the quality of their professional
demeanor, work habits (such as reliability and thoroughness), and communication skills. Many times this feedback is given in conjunction with evaluation
procedures, but if not, the student should request it.

Ask for Opportunities That Fulfill Learning Needs

Site supervisors typically volunteer for their roles because they want to facilitate
interns' learning. However, supervisors cannot always predict precisely what
experiences might be useful to an intern. It is the intern's responsibility to ask
for help in gaining the experiences they need within the site.

Faculty Supervisor's Roles and Functions

The faculty supervisor has important roles to play in the supervised practice
experience. Depending on the nature and scope of the academic program, there
may be an internship coordinator who has overall administrative responsibility
for the internship component of the program and an individual faculty supervisor to whom interns are assigned, creating joint responsibility for the internship.
In other programs, each major professor is responsible for the internship of
advisees, and there is no overall coordinator. In yet other programs, the supervised practice experience is treated as any other class, with a faculty supervisor
responsible for the instruction and the internship oversight. What follows are
descriptions of the roles that need to be fulfilled to assure high-quality internships. Whether one or several persons fulfill the roles varies from program to
program; there is no best way for managing an internship program.

The faculty supervisor is typically not at the supervised practice work site but should check in with the site supervisor during the experience. In addition, the roles described next also need to be filled; interns should seek clarification from the faculty in their program if it is unclear who fills each role. Faculty supervisor roles include the following:

- Placement facilitator—works with student and the site to set up the supervised practice experience
- Sounding board—consults with student and site supervisor throughout the experience
- Intellectual challenger—asks the student challenging questions and assists him or her in applying theory to practice
- Conflict intermediary—serves as a mediator when issues arise that cannot be settled between the student and those at the supervised practice site
- Provider of emotional support—processes the supervised practice experience with the student beyond just task accomplishment
- Information resource—communicates timely and appropriate information to all supervised practice stakeholders
- Assignor of grades—submits the official assessment of the supervised practice experience to the institution

The faculty supervisor's first responsibility is to assist interns in locating suitable placements. A variety of techniques are used effectively in coordinating this matching process and attaining formal agreements with site supervisors. In some programs, interns are provided a list of approved sites and are instructed to contact site supervisors to inquire about placement—similar to a job search. In other cases, interns are expected to locate a suitable site and negotiate the terms of the experience with the faculty and site supervisors. (Sites may use a number of techniques for selecting interns, from formal application processes to informal interviews. Some sites may be highly competitive; others may be open to all students who are interested.) Other programs assign students to sites, generally based on expressions of interest by students.

Whatever process is used, the faculty supervisor's responsibility is to determine whether (a) there is a qualified site supervisor who is willing to have an intern for the particular term; (b) the functional area's practice conforms to the Council for the Advancement of Standards in Higher Education (CAS) standards closely enough that students will be exposed to sound student affairs practices; (c) there are adequate facilities and support to accommodate an intern; and (d) the site supervisor is willing to comply with the terms of the internship agreement (e.g., provide regular individual supervision, assign and evaluate relevant projects). It is also the faculty supervisor's responsibility to make sure that the site supervisor understands the academic program's goals for the internship experience and the expectations of students and site supervisors.

Faculty supervisors and interns should maintain regular contact throughout the internship. This may be accomplished in a number of ways: e-mail activity logs, synchronous and asynchronous interactions, or regular seminar meetings with interns. No matter what the means, the faculty supervisor functions as a sounding board. Interns should use the contacts to ask questions that they do not feel comfortable broaching with the site supervisor, put forth ideas for feedback before presenting them in the placement site, and request organizational history that can help the intern understand the unit's dynamics. Faculty supervisors also can be useful in helping interns analyze their feelings and reactions related to events that occur in the site. Sometimes interns encounter difficulties at the site and need someone to simply listen; faculty supervisors can often fulfill this role.

Faculty supervisors also function as intellectual challengers. Through regular contacts with interns, they challenge students to relate what they have learned in the classroom to what they see happening in the internship site. One of the more difficult tasks students have is relating theory to practice. Because of the type of professional preparation received or the extent of continuing education they have experienced, site supervisors may have difficulty in assisting students to understand how theory is used in daily practice. Faculty supervisors help students verbalize how they see theory applying and identify situations or instances when the theory does not seem to apply and explore why.

Occasionally, interns become involved in conflict situations with site supervisors, other site staff, student-clients, or staff in other institutional units. If the conflict situation becomes too severe, faculty supervisors may be called on to mediate the situation. Faculty supervisors, however, generally resist becoming directly involved because they are not informed about all the factors involved (usually hearing only the intern's perspective), and because it generally is a much better learning experience for interns when they devise ways to resolve their own conflicts. Interns, however, should not hesitate to inform their faculty supervisors when they encounter conflict, but they also should not expect the faculty supervisor to solve their problems for them. Most faculty supervisors defer direct intervention until the intern and his or her site supervisor have unsuccessfully attempted to resolve the conflict.

Faculty supervisors often provide emotional support to interns as they work through difficult or challenging situations. Interns, especially early in their placement, are often called upon to perform tasks they have never attempted before and that may cause uncomfortably heightened anxiety. Faculty supervisors often provide encouragement, reassurance, and succor since interns are required to function more independently than they have been required to do in the classroom. As interns gain self-confidence and experience successes in the internship, they generally need less emotional support from others.

Another role that faculty supervisors play is that of information resource. Frequently, students encounter questions or are given assignments that require research in the literature. If the typical bibliographic aids such as ERIC do not produce sufficient resources, interns often consult their faculty supervisor for advice in the search process. Because faculty members are ordinarily fairly conversant with the field's literature, they can point interns toward potentially useful information.

The final role that faculty supervisors play is that of assigning grades for the internship course. Because faculty members are charged with the responsibility of upholding the academic integrity and standards of the institution, they are the ones with the ultimate responsibility for assigning grades for the internship. In most instances, grades are based on accomplishment of the objectives specified in the learning contract, quality of performance on assignments (e.g., research or other kinds of projects), completion of assignments made by the site supervisor, attendance in the site, and the recommendation of the site supervisor.

Site Staff Members

Some of the most important allies and resources an intern can have are the staff members at the site. Often some of these individuals have been employed at the institution for several years and have institutional memory that can provide useful insight into the operation of the organization. They generally are rich sources of information, can informally advise interns who to see for what, and especially know what the best approach is to different offices or staff members. Frequently, the staff members on many campuses have an effective informal communication network that is better (or at least faster) than formal official communication. Staff members also can be effective instructors for interns about the informal (unwritten) rules of the workplace—for instance, in some settings staff members are expected to eat lunch away from their workspace; in other offices there is a tradition of dressing in business casual clothing on Fridays. Because functional unit staff members may be more immediately accessible than site supervisors, they can answer many questions about the institution or unit in a more timely way than the supervisor.

Even though it is important to develop friendly relationships with members of the staff, there are several potential pitfalls to avoid.

- Avoid the perception of competition or invasion of territory. Interns need to be sensitive about how they are perceived by the other staff. It is essential that staff members not be threatened by interns taking over responsibilities normally delegated to the staff. If staff members come to view the intern as someone who could take their jobs, they are likely to react defensively to the intern. This is especially true in units that do not host interns regularly.
- Do not become involved in personal lives. Frequently, interns spend a considerable amount of time with the staff. Through this constant interaction staff members may come to view the intern as someone with whom they can share their personal problems. Interns are advised to avoid becoming enmeshed in staff members' personal lives. If that should happen, the potential for learning from the internship experience may be greatly diminished.
- Do not become a go-between. If the staff and their supervisor are having difficulty in communicating, it may be tempting for staff to seek to use

the intern as messenger to the boss. Interns are advised to avoid becoming entangled in these kinds of problems, even if it appears that staff members have legitimate concerns or grievances.

• Keep roles clarified. Interns are *special* in that they function as professional staff members on some occasions and as students on others. Because of the shifts between these roles, other staff members may be confused about the degree of authority an intern has in the role. Interns have greater flexibility of work schedules and may have privileges related to their educational status, such as having lunch with the senior professionals or time away from work during academic breaks, that staff members do not enjoy. Because of their role as learners, interns may be asked to question or evaluate certain practices when the staff is not afforded the same opportunity. These differences in authority, responsibility, and access to decision makers can lead to resentment by the staff unless interns frequently make their role and purpose as a learner transparent. Even though interns do some of the same kinds of work as others in the setting, the intern's primary reason for being there is to enhance understanding of the functional area and the field, not just to ease the workload in the office. Ideally, both goals can be realized in the internship.

Students and Other Clientele

Interns sometimes encounter problematic situations when working with students and others who constitute a site's clientele. Potential difficulties include (a) resolving confusion about role and authority, (b) conveying a professional approach, (c) working within the structure, and (d) disclosing personal relationships.

Resolving Confusion About Role and Authority

Students and others who are the clientele of a particular unit often have difficulty understanding the role and authority of a graduate student. Is a graduate student viewed as another professional staff member? Or are they more like the student users of the services and programs? When can the graduate student make independent decisions? When should students or other clients seek decisions directly from the supervisor or other staff members?

When the supervised practice student first arrives in the site, the supervisor can clarify the situation by carefully explaining to staff members exactly what role the intern will play in the organization. It is also important that the intern explain their responsibilities clearly to colleagues and clients. However, these actions may not completely eliminate troublesome situations, since students and other clients may resist seeing the intern in a professional role. The following Reflection Activity encourages critical thinking about responses to questions regarding interns' role and authority.

Reflection Activity

Directions: Read the case and decide how Jasmine should respond.

Jasmine has been at her internship in the Alumni Office for several weeks. One of her tasks is to plan three information sessions called "Changes and Challenges at the University" during the homecoming activities for young alumni. Although the supervisor has explained Jasmine's role to Justin, the president of the young alumni organization, Justin will not respond to Jasmine's requests for information and dialogue. Instead, whenever Jasmine e-mails a request to Justin, he initiates a dialogue with the supervisor. As a result, it is taking Jasmine much longer to complete her tasks, and she is worried that she won't meet the timeline she established to plan a high-quality event.

How should Jasmine respond to this situation?

Conveying a Professional Image

To be effective, graduate interns need to be able to establish professional working relationships with all clients who have contact with the student affairs unit. Student clients may see the intern as no different from them, and some other clients may view the graduate student as too inexperienced to be helpful or effective. It is important, therefore, that graduate interns convey a professional approach in a variety of ways. The following are some behaviors to think about when establishing oneself as a professional in a new setting:

- *Dress.* The overall formality of campuses and offices varies greatly. In some settings, wearing a tie is the norm for men, for example, and in others attire is much more casual. The best approach is to match the type of dress worn by professional colleagues.
- *Communications.* With the advent of texting, it is tempting to write e-mails or messages to clients without attention to standard written English. However, making sure that written communications are friendly but businesslike will do much to communicate a professional demeanor. Verbal communications can also be troublesome. Using overly formal language can be perceived as arrogant and less than inviting, particularly to student clients. On the other hand, use of the current slang (especially swear words) or overly casual language might be appropriate with friends, but not in a professional context.
- *Social media.* Students and other clients are likely to see the social media presence of staff members—even when privacy settings are in place. Therefore, it is important that all staff are intentional about what is posted on

Facebook or similar sites. Graduate interns in supervised practice would be well advised to avoid posting any material that could be seen as unethical or unprofessional. Also, it is important for interns to work with supervisors to determine whether to invite clients to participate in their social media accounts (e.g., Facebook, Twitter).

Working Within an Established Structure

Usually, the clients that interact most frequently with the site have established ways of doing things, with entrenched communication patterns and relationships with particular staff members. Interns need to be careful that they do not inadvertently disrupt these established ways of operating. Many of these norms serve useful purposes, such as maintaining continuity between clients and staff, creating predictable communications, and reducing ambiguity around job responsibilities. Consequently, interns should seek information about the history, context, and dynamics of a situation before jumping in to resolve a problem. The following Reflection Activity demonstrates a lack of contextual knowledge on the part of the intern.

Reflection Activity

Harry has an assistantship in the Student Activities Office at a large public university. His responsibilities include advising the Council of Presidents of the largest student organizations. After Harry's first meeting with the Council, Jane (president of the Student Activities Board) asks Harry's support to ask for an additional allocation from the student government to hire a consultant to provide leadership training to the Board members. After Jane explains some of the serious decision-making and accountability problems experienced by the Board, Harriet agrees that more high-quality leadership training would be needed and offers to write a letter of support for Jane's request.

What Harriet doesn't know is that other members do not share Jane's interpretation of the Board's problems. Other members of the Board see the problem as one of Jane's inept leadership. Also the university's Leadership Development Office is already developing a system of staff consultants to assist in situations such as this.

1.   What are some possible results of Harry's decision to write the letter of support? With the student government? With the Student Activities Board? With the Leadership Development Office?
2.   How might Harry have more effectively addressed Jane's request?

Disclosing Personal Information

When working with a student or other client, it is often tempting for graduate students to tell their own story about a similar situation. This type of self-disclosure does create a bond with the client; students, in particular, tend to want to know the details of a graduate student's life. However, there are risks to sharing too much information.

1. The client can easily misinterpret the relationship as a friendship rather than a professional relationship. True friends are equal in terms of power in the relationship; they feel free to share intimate details of their lives; they often keep each other's problems or lapses quiet, even when it is in the best interest of the workplace to honestly address these; and there is less likelihood of negative feedback and constructive disagreement for fear of disrupting the friendship. When a professional relationship evolves into a companionable friendship, the growth of the student, the growth of the intern, and the progress of the office are all compromised.
2. Too much personal disclosure takes the focus off the student or client's issues. It may seem that telling a story of the graduate student's similar experience would be helpful by putting forth ideas for resolution or building a deeper bond with the student. Yet these good intentions are often lost with too much emphasis on the graduate intern's experiences. Most simply, valuable time is wasted with too much storytelling by the graduate student. Furthermore, what one thinks is a similar situation to the issue presented by the student or client is often built on assumptions—about background experiences, the context of the situation, the intentions of others involved in the issue—that may be erroneous and, more importantly, could be perceived as highly disrespectful. The following Reflection Activity illustrates this point.

Reflection Activity

John has an assistantship in the Residential Life Office where he is the hall director for a small living-learning community focused on social justice. John is a new graduate student who is White and has a highly successful undergraduate leadership background. The living-learning community has an upcoming project to spend a weekend working at a soup kitchen and activities center for Mexican migrant workers. One of the leaders of the community, Caesar (who is also a student leader of the Latin American Cultural Center), has been unusually quiet in the planning sessions for this event.

John decides to talk with Caesar about why he is so quiet. John shares a story from his own experience where he was nervous and scared about a community service project where those being served were homeless and poor.

John told Caesar that he should just "put himself out there" and approach those migrant workers with a friendly attitude.

Caesar told John that his reluctance was not because of nervousness about being around people different from himself; instead, he was worried that the members of the living-learning community did not have enough prior training. Caesar envisioned members of the community saying things that could be seen as microaggressions and that his university peers could focus on the deficits of the workers rather than their strengths. Caesar shares that his grandparents were migrant workers and sometimes were helped by volunteers who were less than respectful. Answer the following questions:

1.   What are some assumptions John is making?
2.   How might John have prevented this situation?

Troubleshooting the Internship: Advice for Interns

As with most professional endeavors, no internship is perfect. There are always problems or issues that need to be resolved. The following sections address some problems or issues that interns frequently encounter and provide some suggestions for avoiding or dealing with them.

Poor Match With Supervisor

It is impossible to match all interns' and supervisors' personalities and work styles. Interns must simply accept the fact that these differences exist and that in the world of work one must learn to work cooperatively with all types of people. Instead of being angry or resentful, interns should concentrate on being productive and learning what characteristics of supervision are not a good match for future positions. Consult the faculty supervisor about possible strategies that can be used to create a more helpful situation.

The Vanished Supervisor

Frequently, students seek out internship sites based in large measure on the good reputation a site supervisor may have established based on work with students, inventiveness of programs, personal magnetism, or past supervision of interns. Because of the importance of the supervisory relationship, these may be good reasons for seeking placement in a particular site or at a given institution. Yet sometimes an intern will discover that—because of circumstances such as job change—the supervisor whom the student sought is no longer available by the time she or he is ready to begin the internship. This also may happen to new professionals when taking their first positions.

The situation has the potential of becoming a major problem for the student. When the initial supervisor leaves the site on short notice or assumes other duties that preclude following through with the planned supervision, then there may be issues of who, if anyone, is qualified and available to supervise the internship. We caution students to try to keep the situation in perspective and resist the temptation to allow the disappointment to interfere with efforts to make the placement site the best learning situation possible.

We suggest that the student immediately discuss the issues with the faculty supervisor and the originally intended site supervisor (if possible). Students should resist the temptation to immediately withdraw from the setting before they explore alternative arrangements for supervision and discuss the situation with the faculty supervisor and possibly with the new site supervisor if one has been identified. In some instances and depending on timing, it may be best to talk with a faculty supervisor about changing the site for the supervised practice experience.

Unfortunately, we cannot offer foolproof solutions to these predicaments. The faculty supervisor is likely to be the student's best resource in deciding whether to seek another site or in creating a new plan that can salvage the learning potential of the altered situation. The faculty supervisor may need to assume a more active role in helping the replacement supervisor understand the purpose of the internship and the academic program's expectations of supervisors, interns, and placement sites.

The Absent Supervisor

For a variety of reasons, supervisors may simply spend little time in their offices during certain periods; this may be typical or may be the result of unusual circumstances. In either case, it can become a significant concern for interns. The faculty supervisor should be consulted so that the supervised practice experience can be modified to assure that the student gets appropriate guidance moving forward.

The Overwhelmed Supervisor

Even with the best of intentions, sometimes supervisors become overwhelmed with work or personal or family problems that severely limit their opportunities to interact with interns. If this is not a short-term situation, inquire about getting additional supervision from another professional at the site. It also may be necessary to informally seek out others in the setting who can provide appropriate feedback and guidance. It is also important that the intern consult with the faculty supervisor if the lack of site supervision is negatively affecting the learning opportunities.

Too Much or Too Few Responsibilities

An important part of negotiating the supervised practice experience is establishing a mutually agreed-upon set of learning objectives and possible outcomes.

Yet some students express concern about being given more work to do than could possibly be accomplished in the time frame of the experience. Interns may be fearful of confronting the issue with the site supervisor for a variety of reasons, including a bad evaluation. However, being honest and asking supervisors about priorities and what tasks should be handled first may help eliminate this problem. A conversation with the site supervisor may also help the student learn more efficient ways to approach a work task.

The opposite situation can also arise where a student is not given enough work to do at the site. All jobs have an ebb and flow of activity dependent of time of year, needs of users of the service or program, or institutional priorities. It is important for the intern to not allow too much time to pass with little to do before bringing it to the attention of the supervisor. Supervised practice is time limited, so it is important to confront any issue fairly soon after it begins, or students lose valuable time in the learning process.

Dual Relationships

Dual relationships in this context are those in which the intern and supervisor form kinds of relationships other than supervisory. For example, these relationships can be friendships, romantic, sexual, or financial. In all of these cases, the line between intern and supervisor and other kinds of relationships becomes blurred. If an intern wants to form a friendship with his or her supervisor, or has romantic interests, or wants to form a business arrangement, the intern is best advised to wait until the internship has been completed. This also applies to dual relationships with other staff member or student users of the programs or services of the internship site. For a more complete discussion of this topic, see Chapter 5.

Fear of Disclosing Mistakes

Sometimes interns are reticent to reveal mistakes they have made to their supervisors because they fear this will be used against them or will lower their grades. Even though it may be uncomfortable, generally, it is not wise to keep mistakes from supervisors because it limits the potential learning and may result in the intern never fully developing his or her potential to be a competent or even outstanding professional practitioner. Most of the leaders in the field with whom we are acquainted can enumerate a long list of mistakes from which they learned important lessons. If interns think or feel that they have made mistakes, even if they are not sure, the best course of action is to discuss possible mistakes with site supervisors as quickly as possible and to offer to take corrective action as soon as possible.

Interns should also be aware that there are some kinds of mistakes that cannot be repaired. The kinds of mistakes that would lead to termination of an employee can also lead to the termination of an internship. It is important for interns and supervisors to specifically discuss the types of problem behaviors that are major deviations from expectations in the particular office or university culture. Some of the kinds of behavior that typically fall into this category include (a) violations of professional ethical standards, (b) acts of violence against others, (c) violations of the criminal code, (d) behavior that is damaging to the reputation or functioning of the unit or the institution, (e) violation of unit or institutional policy, (f) violation of safety regulations or policies, (g) violation of the dress code, (h) failure to perform assigned duties, (i) excessive tardiness or unacceptable absences, and (j) insubordination (failure to do as told by legitimate authority).

Interns should also remember that it may be a much more serious offense to attempt to conceal or lie about a situation than it would be to reveal and discuss the situation openly and honestly. Many supervisors will forgive errors but will not accept lying or deceit. Almost without exception, mistakes made, acknowledged, and corrected during the internship result only in positive learning.

Doing Menial Tasks

From time to time, interns in most settings are called upon to do time-consuming, mundane chores, such as answering the telephone, making copies, stuffing envelopes, or filing. Several things need to be kept in mind when this happens. First, at times of high pressure or crisis, staff at all levels can be expected to pitch in and get tasks done. Second, if these tasks are not done correctly, an office's reputation can be sullied and cause a loss of credibility with its clients. Even though tedious, completing the task well is also important. Third, even though necessary to accomplishment of the site's goals, this kind of work by itself has limited educational value for interns.

If interns feel that they are frequently asked to do work unrelated to the agreed-upon learning goals, then they should discuss the concerns with the site supervisor. It may be useful to remind the supervisor about the learning goals established for the internship and to respectfully inquire how the menial tasks promote goal accomplishment. If difficulties of this nature persist, then it should be discussed with the faculty supervisor.

Conclusion

Internship supervision is a key ingredient in the ultimate success of students in preparation for their professions. Because this experience serves to help students integrate all of their learning experiences in their preparation program, its quality goes a long way in defining success for the student. When the internship is accomplished successfully, interns generally feel that their preparation programs have also fulfilled their educational goals. Certainly, internship supervision is vital to this process.

Quality supervision is about promoting learning with student interns. Central to this process is building relationships, especially between the site supervisor and the student intern. Other relationships are important also, such as with the faculty supervisor, support staff in the site, and student clients. When these relationships are built on solid ground, interns generally are successful. They learn what they need to learn to feel self-confident in their abilities, and they fully integrate all of their learning experiences.

Building appropriate relationships is developmental and can be characterized in stages that reflect intern needs, tasks to be accomplished by interns, and supervision strategies. These stages depict steps in relationship building from entrée to saying good-bye to site supervisors.

Just as internships are full of learning opportunities, they also can be fraught with difficulties. These opportunities and difficulties have been discussed in this chapter with a view toward helping interns see ways in which they can play major roles in the ultimate success of the internship experience.

References

Chiaferi, R., & Griffin, M. (1997). *Developing fieldwork skills: A guide for human services, counseling, and social work students.* Pacific Grove, CA: Brooks/Cole.

Gutierrez, P., Metzger, M., Chandrashekar, N., Carter, D., Hawes, C., Springate, B., Saunders, S., & Allen, G. (2010). *Assessment of supervision competencies among student affairs professionals.* Unpublished manuscript, University of Connecticut.

Kiser, P. M. (2013). *The human services internship: Getting the most from your experience.* Belmont, CA: Brooks/Cole.

Kuh, G. D., Siegel, M. J., & Thomas, A. D. (2001). Higher education: Values and culture. In R. B. Winston, Jr., D. G. Creamer, T. K. Miller, & Associates (Eds.), *The professional student affairs administrator: Educator, leader, and manager* (pp. 39–63). New York, NY: Brunner-Routledge.

Tull, T. A., Hirt, J. B., & Saunders, S. A. (2009). Implications and recommendations. In T. A. Tull, J. B. Hirt, & S. A. Saunders (Eds.), *Becoming socialized in student affairs administration: A guide for new professionals and supervisors* (pp. 127–154). Sterling, VA: Stylus.

Winston, R. B., Jr., & Creamer, D. G. (1997). *Improving staffing practices in student affairs.* San Francisco, CA: Jossey-Bass.

4   The Evaluation Process

Evaluation of learning and performance should be an ongoing process in the supervised practice experience. With the increased emphasis in student affairs during the past 30 years on assessment and evaluation, a culture now exists where these processes are no longer viewed just as end of activity events (Schuh, 2013). In keeping with this change in conceptualization, this chapter will explore the evaluation process as an ongoing set of activities that will help students maximize learning in the supervised practice experience.

For all supervised practice experiences, the evaluation processes should be ongoing rather than a single summative event at the end of the experience. Since internships are typically 8 to 16 weeks in duration, it is especially important that the evaluation process begins early, in some cases prior to the first day of work. Position descriptions, developed before the intern is selected, drive the development of learning objectives, learning contracts, and supervisory agreements, which are useful in assessing the work experience (the development of these tools is discussed in Chapter 2). Once the intern is selected, these items should be revisited and modified so agreement on the criteria to be used for evaluation is achieved. During the supervised practice experience, there should be both informal and formal processes of reporting and reflecting on the experiences and skill development. Formally, these processes should include consideration of how a student applies theories and concepts learned in the classroom to the internship activities (Everett, Miehl, DuBois, & Garran, 2011). Other methods discussed here include competency analysis and reflection journals. Finally, the end of a supervised practice experience typically includes an evaluation of performance and skill development, as well as an assessment of learning outcome accomplishment. Each of these components of evaluation will be discussed in this chapter.

Evaluating the Experience

The main focus of internships, practica, and other site-based experiences is linking theory with practice, a foundational concept of the student affairs profession. The link between theory and practice, however, does not always appear obvious or occur automatically (Jaeger, Dunstan, Thornton, Rockenbach, Gayles, & Haley, 2013; Love, 2012). Often, purposeful and intentional activities are necessary to completely process the application of theory, both formal and informal, to student affairs practice.

One way this can occur is for students to function as reflective practitioners who understand their strengths, weaknesses, preferences, and learning styles, as well as the specifics of the theories and concepts (Reason & Kimball, 2012). Most importantly, a reflective practitioner uses his or her own appraisal as a central source of data in determining the effectiveness of performance and relationships. As the supervised practice continues, students collect data from a variety of sources that can be helpful in all aspects of the evaluative process. These data may include information from events, such as program evaluation forms, or feedback from users of the functional unit, such as students or parents.

Even though incorporating evaluation feedback from site and faculty supervisors is essential, depending totally on others to appraise the supervised practice performance produces an incomplete picture that misses the rich, detailed information about individual learning that only the student can provide. Interns' personal appraisals of the supervised practice experience should include both formative and summative approaches.

Formative Assessment

Formative evaluation is designed to provide ongoing check-in and feedback activities. Throughout the course of the internship, students should keep track of their accomplishments and should regularly monitor achievement of previously agreed-upon learning objectives. There should be a formal and informal process to reflect on progress and personal reactions to what is seen, heard, and experienced (Kiser, 2013). The site or faculty supervisor may have already developed a procedure that fosters this type of broad and meaningful reflection. Regular supervision as well as internship class meetings throughout the experience should provide opportunities for this type of formative assessment to occur.

Students involved in supervised practice experiences also benefit from meeting formally and informally with other students to discuss what they are learning and receive peer feedback regarding their personal assessment. This can be during the formal course time or with small groups that meet outside of class time. Without some type of interactive activity, students could fail to recognize the interrelationships between the experience, theories, personal knowledge, and individual professional values.

There is great value in recording reflections and in sharing them with a more experienced professional. The structure of writing and sharing helps most interns stay focused on this important process. The reflection journal (presented in Appendix 4) is an excellent way to foster the broad, meaningful reflection advocated throughout the supervised practice experience. It is crucial, however, that students take the time to complete their journals thoughtfully and on a regular basis. Simply putting down the tasks one accomplished without thinking through the implications is merely making a list, not engaging in reflection. Though it will take dedication to complete the reflection journal regularly, the information recorded will be useful as the internship is ending and final summative evaluation material is created.

Reflection journals may or may not be shared with site supervisors. At times, an honest reflection may contain material that a student does not want to share with a supervisor when the relationship is of short duration or when trust is not yet developed. In this situation, the students' reflection journal acts as repository of personal thoughts, accomplishments, and questions to ask during one-on-one supervision time. At a minimum, though, students should be writing a report to the site supervisor on a weekly basis that outlines (a) progress on learning goals, (b) challenges, and (c) questions that need answering.

We recommend that students share the reflection journal in its entirety with the faculty supervisor, however. The responsibility of a faculty supervisor is to help students make meaning of their experiences and to integrate theory, practice, and personal and professional development. Sharing broad, meaningful reflections with a faculty member who is knowledgeable about theories and professional development strategies provides students with a powerful opportunity to maximize their learning from the internship.

Summative Evaluation

The summative evaluation at the close of the supervised practice experience is an important learning opportunity as well. The foundation of a summative evaluation of the internship effectiveness depends not on the supervisor's evaluation but on the student's own reflective answers to crucial questions, such as these:

1. To what extent did I achieve the learning goals established at the beginning of the internship?
2. What personal attributes helped me achieve my goals?
3. What elements of my work environment (e.g., supervisor, office staff, office structure) helped me achieve my goals?
4. What personal attributes, attitudes, or behaviors hindered me in achieving my goals? How might the outcomes been different if I had acted or felt differently?
5. What elements of the work environment impeded my progress in achieving my goals?

6. How would I analyze my work performance? Am I being a reliable employee who is being ethical in my actions? Am I completing projects I am assigned?
7. Do I meet or exceed the expectations of my site supervisor? If so, how? If not, why not?
8. What did I learn from the site supervisor's and colleagues' feedback about strengths and weaknesses as a new student affairs practitioner?
9. With which feedback do I agree? With which feedback do I disagree?
10. What new skills did I acquire through the internship?
11. Did I learn skills that I did not expect to acquire? If so, what were these?
12. What skills do I need or want to strengthen through subsequent professional experiences?
13. What are at least three things that I learned that I should never do again?

These reflective questions need to be answered at the conclusion of each supervised practice experience. At the end of an internship it is easy for the student to get caught up in rushing to finish last-minute tasks, preparing for final exams, and planning for the next academic term or for a first professional position. In that rush, it is easy to neglect the importance of reflecting on and evaluating the total internship experience. It is important to get in the habit of practicing formative reflection as a normal part of daily activities to avoid missing important points when finishing the supervised practice experience.

ePortfolios

The expansion of technology use has created a tool that has become useful for students in supervised practice experiences. According to Denzine (2001), ePortfolios used in higher education serve a learning purpose as a collection of "student works that exhibit student's effort, progress, and achievements" (p. 497). These can serve both as a repository of examples of work products and as an organizing mechanism for students to make meaning of their task accomplishments. Creating ePortfolios can also provide an opportunity for students to reflect deeply on their learning experiences (Janosik & Frank, 2013), their development, and their professional identity (Rickards et al., 2008). ePortfolios should be considered as a tool to use in the evaluation process (formative and summative).

Analysis of Learning Contracts

In Chapter 2 of this text, the importance of developing a learning contract that included goals and timelines for the supervised practice experience was explained. Typically, these are written and approved early in the internship experience. An important part of the evaluation process should include a complete review of the learning contracts done jointly with the site supervisor. The sample learning contract discussed in Chapter 2 contained specific objectives, activities, skills and competencies, and time requirements for an internship experience. If one now reviewed those objectives from an evaluative standpoint, the following questions could be raised: "Did I accomplish this?" "What was the outcome?" "What evidence do I have that confirms I achieved the outcome?"

The sample contract provided in Appendix 2 specified the following: "Objective 1: To assist with the development of a peer conflict resolution model proposal." Specific activities and time requirements to assist Jane in meeting that objective were listed:

a. Research conflict resolution models of other universities and suggestions from the National Association of Mediation in Education. [20 hours]
b. Meet regularly with the site supervisor to discuss progress. [15 hours]
c. Consult with other Dean of Students Office staff members on model components. [5 hours]

In addition, Jane stated in her "Skills and Competencies to Be Acquired" section that she would hone her research skills, she would learn to tailor various conflict resolution models to a specific institution, and she would develop skills to collaborate effectively with many student affairs professionals.

Reflection Exercise

The following exercise can assist interns to assess the degree to which the learning objectives of their contracts were achieved. As you finish your internship or practicum, complete these four steps:

Step 1: Review each objective and write a specific description of how you met that objective.

Step 2: Note any unanticipated activities that occurred that were not in the original contract.

Step 3: Repeat this process for all objectives.

Step 4: Reflect on the skills and competencies you intended to acquire as a result of the supervised practice experience. You will need to answer in writing the following questions:

1. With which of the skills and competencies am I most confident?
2. What is the evidence that supports this conclusion?
3. Which skills and competencies do I need to further develop?
4. Specifically, what is the evidence that supports this conclusion?

Analysis of Work Performance

Analysis of work performance consists of two parts: (a) the quality of completing tasks assigned and (b) the quality of the student's interactions with students, staff members at the site, supervisors, and external constituents. The learning objectives created at the beginning of the internship should contain many of the tasks to be completed as a part of the internship experience. However, some of the tasks that were completed may have been unanticipated when the internship began. For example, John noted in his learning contract that he planned to design a new leadership program for first-year students. However, once he arrived at the internship site, he discovered that such a program already existed but was not operating in a very visible manner across campus. So, John completed a benchmarking assessment process in which he looked at how other emerging leaders' programs were marketed to first-year students. His assessment included conducting telephone interviews with leadership educators who had developed exemplary programs on other campuses. Even though this assessment was not originally part of the learning objectives, it certainly was a task that consumed time and required development of skills; it should be included as part of the summative evaluation. The following activity outlines the steps that should be taken to complete a personal appraisal of the tasks one has accomplished (Kiser, 2013).

Reflection Activity

Quality of Task Completion

1. Gather information from your weekly journals, your calendar, to-do lists, memos, or notes from your supervisor. Use this information to construct a list of tasks you have accomplished during the internship. Your list of accomplishments should consist of your substantive tasks, not every telephone call made or e-mail message written. Using your journal, calendar, and to-do lists serves to remind you of what you have accomplished, rather than encouraging you to rely on your general memories.

2. For each of the accomplishments you identify, grade your performance using the following scale:
    5 = outstanding, far more proficient than I expected
    4 = good, somewhat more proficient than I expected
    3 = average, about as proficient than I expected
    2 = poor, somewhat less proficient than I expected
    1 = inadequate, much less proficient than I expected

3. For each rating, write a brief, *factually based* statement that supports your rating.

Quality of Interpersonal Relationships

This portion of evaluating your work performance is considerably more subjective and, therefore, likely to be subject to bias. Yet reflecting on how well you interacted with students, colleagues, supervisors, and other constituents is a critical component of the learning process. The ability to collaborate, incorporate feedback, communicate unpopular decisions, meet the needs of clients, and portray a positive attitude are all essential elements of success in higher education administration. The following steps will assist you in reflecting on your strengths and weaknesses of your interactions with others:

1. Identify the categories of individuals you worked with during the course of your internship. These categories are site specific and may include students, colleagues, supervisors, support staff, faculty, or external constituents.

2. For each of the categories, write a short paragraph outlining your successes and challenges or frustrations in dealing with people in this category. Referring to your reflection journal will likely help you in this process. Once you begin to write your paragraphs, you may recognize that a category is too broad to be meaningful. For example, you may have discovered different challenges dealing with student leaders than in working with student employees at your site. If you find that the categories are too broad, divide them into more manageable subgroups. If you are having difficulty identifying successes and challenges, think about feedback that you received since you arrived at the site. Or try to imagine how individuals in each category would describe your ability to establish workable interpersonal relationships.

3. Then review what you have written and summarize your strengths and weaknesses in terms of developing workable interpersonal relationships in your site.

Seeking and Using Feedback

The site and faculty supervisors' evaluations of the intern's performance are critical components of an effective internship. They also happen to be the elements of the experience that cause the most anxiety for interns and supervisors alike. The overall purpose of the supervisory evaluation is to assess achievement of outcomes and performance quality. The supervisory evaluation is designed to examine the experience as a whole, identifying strengths and weaknesses (Alle-Corliss & Alle-Corliss, 2005). Even though students should have received regular feedback about their day-to-day performance from the supervisor, the final evaluation allows the supervisor and student to identify patterns, themes, and issues that emerged during the course of the internship. It may also present an opportunity for the site supervisor to further explain the reasoning behind the evaluation.

It is part of the obligation of professionals to evaluate the performance of those who work for them. In fact, the American College Personnel Association Statement of Ethical Principles and Standards (2006) mandated in Section 3.10 that professionals "evaluate job performance of subordinates regularly and recommend appropriate actions to enhance professional development and improve performance."

The critical question, then, is how to prepare for the summative evaluation by the site supervisor and, if appropriate, the faculty supervisor. Evaluation is most productive when it is viewed as a process where students take responsibility for honestly appraising their own performance. It is also important to remember that if students desire to grow professionally, they need to seek out both positive and negative feedback. The internship is the best place to begin establishing a productive approach to evaluation. The preceding sections provide a basis for preparing for student self-evaluation. The following steps will help students prepare for their supervisor's evaluation.

Reflection Activity

1. Review your analysis of learning objectives and your appraisal of your work performance (both of which you completed through the previous exercises).

2. Review the evaluation instrument that your site supervisor will use to complete your summative evaluation. Tell your supervisor that you would like to rate yourself on that instrument so that you can better understand any areas of congruence or discrepancy.

3. Rate your own performance using this instrument and write a few facts that support each of your ratings.

4. At your evaluation conference, discuss discrepancies and similarities between your supervisor's ratings and your ratings.

5. After the evaluation conference is complete, take a few minutes to summarize the conversation so you will remember the major points of your discussion. Reflect on what actions you tried to take to make the evaluation conference successful. Finally, suggest to yourself ways that you could act or attitudes you could adopt that would make future evaluation conferences more productive.

Analysis of Skills Developed

Although students likely identified in their learning objectives some of the skills they wanted to develop as a result of the supervised practice experience, the summative evaluation process is a time when students can look at all of the skills they acquired, even those they did not anticipate at the outset. There are several sets of skills that students are likely to want to reflect on. The *ACPA and NASPA Professional Competencies for Student Affairs Professionals* (2010) is an excellent resource to use as a guide in identifying important skill sets at three different levels of expertise necessary for informed practice. The basic level of competency outlined in this document can provide an excellent reference point to assess skill development.

The purpose of assessing skill development is to identify the broad, transferable competencies that have been acquired during the supervised practice experience. Rather than focusing on the specific work tasks or the quality of interpersonal relationships, the assessment of transferable skills requires that one think more globally, synthesizing different elements of the internship experience (Lock, 2005). It is critically important to identify transferable skills since they are what students can highlight in a job interview or cover letter. Simply saying, "I am good with computers" is not sufficient. One needs to be specific, stating, for example, that in the admissions office internship "I learned how to create voice-over PowerPoint presentations that can be uploaded for synchronous or asynchronous webinars." The following structure may help students reflect on the transferable skills acquired and how to communicate them in concrete terms.

Reflective Activity

1. Review your learning objectives, the position description for your internship, your analysis of work performance, results of your site and faculty supervisors' evaluations, and your own self-rating on the supervisory evaluation form.

2. Consult the *ACPA and NASPA Professional Competencies for Student Affairs Professionals* (2010) to make sure you are using reference points considered important to the profession.

3. Review your major internship accomplishments and write them in the far left column of the form that follows.

4. For each of your accomplishments, describe the skills you used. Be certain to state your skills specifically.

5. For each skill, rate your competence using the following scale:
   3 = Very competent
   2 = Somewhat competent
   1 = Minimal or not competent

Table 4.1 Identifying and assessing the skills acquired as a result of my internship example

Accomplishment	Competency achieved (ACPA and NASPA Professional Competencies for Student Affairs Professionals)	Rating
I organized the curriculum for a one-day midyear training program for resident assistants who had served for one semester.	Constructed needs assessment	1
	Analyzed needs assessment data	1
	Researched exemplary programs	2
	Created program theme, learning goals, and topics	3
	Identified and briefed program facilitators	3
	Created participant evaluation form	1

Creating Closure

Although ending an administrative internship is different from ending a counseling-based field placement, the psychological services discipline provides some lessons about how to terminate relationships with clients that also apply to administrative internships. Student affairs interns often form close interpersonal relationships that are difficult to leave. The termination process, therefore, requires special attention to both task and relationship details.

If the supervised practice site is on the same campus as the student's preparation program, the termination of the experience actually can be more difficult than if it is on another campus. This difficulty arises from the fact that the student remains on campus and may experience pressure to complete projects or maintain relationships associated with the site after the formal termination of the internship. Ideally, the student and site supervisor have addressed this issue when establishing learning goals and objectives for the experience, and time limits have been placed on the tasks so that students can leave the site having fulfilled all requirements of the experience. The decision to continue with an unfinished task should be a joint decision of the site supervisor and student that occurs prior to the close of the supervised practice experience. The question of whether the intern continues tasks after the official close of the internship should be decided, with clearly specified parameters, well before the close of the internship.

Unlike colleagues who are counselors, student affairs practitioners typically do not see individual clients or therapeutic groups that require a specialized process for ending the relationship. However, the type of termination of relationships in student affairs still requires that a plan be developed so that all needs are covered, and the site is ready to proceed without the intern's presence. Sweitzer and King (2013) noted that thought should be given to the manner with which an intern ends relationships with students or clients in the functional unit. Again, if the supervised practice experience is on the home campus, the termination process may differ but should be negotiated by the student and site supervisor early in the experience. For example, an intern, Tarek, has been asked to prepare for welcome week as part of his internship experience that officially ends August 1. New students do not actually arrive on campus until August 13, and welcome week is August 13–20. Even though Tarek's learning goals did not stipulate that he would participate in these activities, he may elect to be a volunteer for all or some of those events. In this case, Tarek's termination process would be different from that of someone who is permanently leaving a site.

The first step in the departure process is for the intern to compile a list of all projects or tasks with which she or he has been involved since arriving at the site. An example of a series of steps and activities one might use to prepare to end the supervised practice experience is provided in Appendix 4. A detailed description of projects should include not only the task but also other staff who worked on the task and their roles as well. Once the list is complete, students should identify the parts of each project that have been completed and the steps that will follow. Interns should include the names of individuals who will take responsibility for any next steps so the supervisor will know which people to approach for the continuation of the project. It would be helpful to provide any impressions about the project that will be useful to the supervisor in making any additional assignments to permanent staff. The interns should also be sure to set up a meeting with the supervisor near the end of the supervised practice experience to review this list and answer any additional questions the supervisor might have. Interns should leave a good record of what was done, what is to be done, and identification of possible trouble spots. It is also important to keep copies of correspondence and a record of persons contacted about the activities, with telephone numbers and e-mail addresses.

Likewise, it is also important to carefully consider ways to say goodbye to students and colleagues at the work site. A number of authors who have explored field experience processes have discussed the importance of closure through rituals. Baird (2013) noted that ritual adds a sense of *specialness* to the event and allows for a formal way to recall the value of the experience to the intern and important others from the site.

Closure With the Site Supervisor

The relationship one develops with a site supervisor is often closely tied to the overall success of the supervised practice experience. As with any supervisory relationship, it can be positive and life affirming or negative and inhibiting. Usually, even if the relationship has been less than ideal, the intern has learned something about him- or herself in the process that, with reflection, can be used in the future.

Sweitzer and King (2013) recommended that closure with the site supervisor not only revolve around task status and work performance evaluation but also include time to discuss lessons learned during the experience. The learning goals and objectives identified in the contract can be used as a starting point for this discussion. Many interns, however, find that the greatest lessons they learned during the experience could not necessarily be anticipated. These unexpected learning opportunities might include resolving a conflict, taking a risk, or adapting to an unplanned event. It is important to have time to process these experiences with the site supervisor prior to ending the supervised learning experience to provide a sense of context for the event that will serve the student. Interns should also consider scheduling time to provide the site supervisor with feedback about the experience. This might include exploring what went well during the experience, providing examples of how the experience could be improved for those who will serve as interns in the future, and offering feedback about the supervision received. The latter of these suggestions comes with a word of caution: Students may want to give feedback to the supervisor *only if* the supervisor has asked for that feedback, and the relationship is such that it will be received nondefensively. Students often have concerns that supervisors still have some degree of power in the relationship due to the fact that they may be providing a grade for the experience or letters of recommendation in the future. It is best to let the level of trust and strength of the relationship be the guide when making any decision to provide constructive feedback to a supervisor.

Closure with the Faculty Supervisor

Students also have specific responsibilities related to the classroom component of the supervised practice. In addition to the evaluation components already discussed, students may be asked to complete an assessment of the site. This information can be useful in making decisions about the adequacy of the site for future placements. An example of a site evaluation instrument is included in Appendix 5.

Final Points to Consider About Departure

As interns plan to leave the site, it is important to remember that coworkers during this experience may have invested time and energy into creating the learning opportunity for interns. Typically, they have assisted the interns without financial compensation. Many supervisors believe they have an obligation to give back to the profession through serving as site supervisors in much the same way that someone assisted them when they were in a preparation program. Others see the opportunity to serve as a way to teach skills and competencies they view as important for the continuation of the profession. For most individuals, supervising interns is a form of professional generativity, and as such they take great personal pride in the students' accomplishments and blame themselves for any bad experiences.

Students should check with their faculty supervisor about customs and rituals of leaving internship sites. It is always appropriate to send a thank you letter(s) right after leaving the site to your supervisor and those at the site who have invested in the internship. Students should not let too much time pass between ending the internship and corresponding with the individuals at the host site. Sometimes students also give small tokens of appreciation to their supervisor. Again, interns need to check with the faculty supervisor or others as to what would be considered appropriate in this type of situation.

One other task to accomplish prior to departing an internship involves talking with the site supervisor. Sweitzer and King (2013) provide some important guidelines regarding references that include some suggestions from Baird (2013) as well. These include the following:

1. Have an initial conversation to determine if the supervisor feels comfortable being a positive reference. Just because someone agrees to write a reference letter or is willing to be contacted, it should not be construed to mean that the communication will be positive and glowing. A less-than-positive communication could hurt a student in a future job search more than no communication at all.
2. In some cases, students may also want to ask other personnel at the site to serve as references in the future. It is important to make the same request to these individuals as you would to the site supervisor.
3. No matter who is asked to write a letter or serve as a reference, it is important for the intern to give the reference a clear description of future career goals and objectives. Doing so will assist the writer in gearing the letter to the student's personal strengths in relation to the career path he or she has in mind. It is also generally a good idea to provide a copy of the résumé to help the writer refresh his or her memory. In that résumé the student needs to provide extra detail about the activities and projects engaged in during the supervised experience.
4. Give plenty of notice to those who are serving as references. For those being listed as references on the résumé, the student needs to provide a list of positions for which the he or she is applying as well as a brief description of specific interests.

Supervisors can be important resources for future job-search processes. Time and attention to making the request during the departure period will pay off in the future.

Planning for the Future

The final step in evaluating the supervised practice experience is to translate reflections into goals and plans for continued professional development. As higher education changes ever more rapidly, continued professional development is not a luxury but a survival strategy. Even though institutions and supervisors support professional development, the ultimate responsibility for professional growth rests with the individual. With the plethora of professional association conferences and workshops, online courses and discussion groups, and each college's or university's professional development offerings, student affairs professionals will need a clear understanding of their learning goals to use their limited continuing education time wisely.

Professional Development Planning

Supervised practice and graduate assistantships often serve as the first professional development experiences for student affairs practice. Carpenter and Stimpson (2007) define professional development as "the career-long process of professional improvement" (p. 275). To use the supervised practice experience as a springboard for the type of future professional development to gain specialized expertise, it is crucial to have specific goals and objectives. The reflective activities described in this chapter constitute the needs assessment data that will allow one to create a long-term professional development plan.

Reflection Activity

1. Review your assessment of skill development. Pay particular attention to the areas rated a 1 or 2 since these may constitute areas that require particular attention.

2. For each skill consider whether that skill is desired. For example, you may have given yourself a low rating of 1 for the skill of planning social events for potential donors. Even though a low rating is accurate, you may decide that you really do not want to work in the development area and have little interest in planning social events. It would be a waste of time, then, to do professional reading and attend workshops concerning event planning for potential donors.

3. Create a list of skills that you want to strengthen in the future. You may need to add a few important skills that were not addressed directly in the internship setting.

4. Prioritize the list, using future career goals as a foundation. Ask yourself what skills are most crucial for success. Also, in prioritizing, pay attention to those competencies that are most lacking. For example, you may decide that even though as a future residence life operations manager you will not need to use teaching skills very often, you feel so inadequate about these skills that they appear high on your list.

5. For each of the prioritized skills, identify several professional development opportunities that might help hone that skill. Be sure to include such activities as reading, research on the Web, participation in a Listserv, and visits to other campuses as well as the more traditional approaches such as conferences, workshops, and courses.

6. Look at skills and opportunities. Create several broad learning goals and construct several objectives for each. Be sure to include deadlines with objectives and show evidence that there is a commitment to start work on some of the objectives immediately.

What About the Next Supervised Practice?

Some students are in preparation programs where they can have multiple supervised experiences at different sites. The reflections from the personal appraisal, site evaluation, skills developed list, and professional development plan all provide excellent information to guide the selection of the next internship site. Internships, as has been stated previously, are rich opportunities for skill development and can serve to position students more advantageously for future full-time professional positions. So it is helpful for students to take some time to think through how the next internship options may further their career. The following questions (adapted from Chiaferi & Griffin, 1997, p. 113) are a useful structure for thinking about future internship options.

1. What student groups, functional areas, or organizational structures might one need to experience to position yourself advantageously for the career search?
2. What type of setting and supervision would allow you to build on strengths and address weaknesses?
3. What new skills, knowledge, or attitudes would you like to learn, and what type of setting might afford the greatest opportunity for you to acquire this learning?
4. What important concerns (if any) were overlooked in the current internship?
5. How might you gather the necessary information about potential internship options?

Conclusion

Student affairs work can be a tremendously rewarding career. For many practitioners, the supervised practice experience serves as one of the formal orientations to the field. Students report that just as they are beginning to feel acclimated to the host institution and the internship site, and are fully equipped to make substantial contributions, they must begin preparing to leave. For some students, the last day of work cannot come fast enough; for others, it is a sad event ending enjoyable activities and good relationships. The supervised practice experience is typical of what many new practitioners encounter when they start their first professional positions. The various aspects of participating in orientation, setting goals, establishing good supervisory relations, and planning for evaluation and feedback are all parts of any new job. What has been learned during this time will serve the student well in the future.

References

Alle-Corliss, L., & Alle-Corliss, R. (2005). *Human services agencies: An orientation to field-work* (2nd ed.). Belmont, CA: Brooks/Cole.

American College Personnel Association (2006). *Statement of ethical principles and standards.* Retrieved from www.myacpa.org/au/documents/EthicsStatement.pdf

American College Personnel Association (ACPA)/National Association of Student Affairs Administrators (NASPA). (2010). *Professional competency areas for student affairs practitioners.* Washington, DC: American College Personnel Association and National Association of Student Personnel Administrators.

Baird, B. N. (2013). *The internship, practicum, and field placement handbook: A guide for the helping professions* (7th ed.). Upper Saddle River, NJ: Pearson.

Carpenter, S., & Stimpson, M. T. (2007). Professionalism, scholarly practice and professional development in student affairs. *NASPA Journal, 44*(2), 265–284.

Chiaferi, R., & Griffin, M. (1997). *Developing fieldwork skills: A guide for human services, counseling, and social work students.* Belmont, CA: Brooks/Cole.

Denzine, G. M. (2001). Making a commitment to professional growth: Realizing the potential of professional portfolios. *NASPA Journal, 38*(4), 495–509.

Everett, J. E., Miehl, D., DuBois, C., & Garran, A. M. (2011). The developmental model of supervision as reflected in the experiences of field supervisors and graduate students. *Journal of Teaching in Social Work, 31*(3), 250–264.

Jaegar, A. J., Dunstan, S., Thornton, C., Rockenbach, A. B., Gayles, J. G., & Haley, K. J. (2013). Put theory into practice. *About Campus, 17*(6), 11–15.

Janosik, S. M., & Frank, T. (2013). Using ePortfolios to measure student learning in a graduate preparation program in higher education, *International Journal of ePortfolio, 3*(1), 13–20.

Kiser, P. M. (2013). The human services internship: *Getting the most from your experience* (6th ed.) Belmont, CA: Wadsworth/Thomson Learning.

Levine, J. (2012). *Working with people: The helping process* (9th ed.). Upper Saddle River, NJ: Pearson.

Lock, R. D. (2005). *Taking charge of your career direction: Career planning guide, Book 1* (5th ed.). Belmont, CA: Wadsworth/Thomson Learning.

Love, P. (2012). Informal theory: The ignored link in theory-to-practice. *Journal of College Student Development, 53*(2), 177–191.

Reason, R. D., & Kimball, E. W. (2012). A new theory-to-practice model for student affairs: Integrating scholarship, context, and reflection. *Journal of Student Affairs Research and Practice, 49*(4), 359–376.

Rickards, W. H., Diez, M. E., Ehley, L., Guilbault, L. F., Loacker, G., Hart, J. R., & Smith, P. C. (2008). Learning, reflection, and electronic portfolios: Stepping toward an assessment practice. *Journal of General Education, 57*(1), 31–50.

Schuh, J. H. (2013). Developing a culture of assessment in student affairs. In J. H. Schuh (Ed.), *Selected contemporary assessment issues* (pp. 89–99). New Directions for Student Services No. 142. San Francisco, CA: Jossey-Bass.

Sweitzer, H. F., & King, M. A. (2013). *The successful internship: Transformation and empowerment* (4th ed.). Belmont, CA: Brooks/Cole.

Part Three

5   Legal and Ethical Issues[1]

Internships and assistantships provide students important opportunities to develop personal frameworks for professional behavior. Most often, guidelines for this behavior are provided through the institutions at which they work and the professional associations to which they belong. While much of what is defined as professional behavior is shaped by the culture of the employing organization, statutes, courts and the decisions they make, and statements of ethics also define a large share of one's professional behavior.

The purpose of this chapter is to highlight a number of important legal and ethical issues that should be addressed early in any supervised experience. By doing so, interns will have a clear understanding of the parameters of acceptable behavior and will be less likely to breach laws and rules that govern professional practice and will not inadvertently stumble into unethical behavior. Field supervisors are also more likely to be more satisfied with student performance. Finally, this review will help students develop greater confidence in discharging their responsibilities and aid interns in more quickly developing a framework for professional practice. Topics reviewed in this chapter include formal and informal working relationships, questions of authority and responsibility, liability issues, liability management, compensation issues, and professional ethics and standards.

Formal and Informal Working Relationships

In large measure, the degree of formality evident in a given work setting and the intern–site supervisor relationship is a matter of personality, personal style, and institutional culture. Some site supervisors feel comfortable with a relatively loosely defined work agenda. Others approach the task of supervising a student's field experience with a more explicitly defined structure and expectations. Similarly, the organizational culture of some institutions dictates that everything be written down and signed in triplicate, whereas administrators at other institutions may operate on a more casual basis.

As explained in some detail in Chapter 3, regardless of the formality of the relationship created, students and their supervisors should mutually agree on the tasks to be completed and the learning experiences that are to take place during the internship. Interns who do not establish clear understandings with their site supervisors at the beginning of their field experience run the risk of discovering near the end of the internship that they have not satisfactorily met the site supervisor's expectations. Even though it is not possible (or even desirable) to specify every minute task or assignment to be performed, a clear understanding documented and agreed upon gives the intern the security of knowing the expectations and frees the site supervisor from the task of having to repeatedly clarify expectations.

In situations where the student is to receive a stipend for the work conducted during the internship, a job description usually identifies the expectations of the supervisor. Absent an employment agreement, other types of documents may serve this purpose. Supervisors may wish to write a letter of appointment or a memorandum of understanding that outlines the nature of the relationship between the student and the supervisor and highlights what is to be accomplished during the course of the internship. In many cases, the professor serving as the faculty supervisor for the course will require that a behavioral contract be developed and agreed upon. This learning contract serves the same purpose (See Chapter 2 for details about learning contracts.).

Regardless of its form, having a document that establishes ground rules for the experience serves to enhance the student's learning and subsequent evaluation. Such a document should include (a) the goals or the educational objectives to be achieved, (b) the specific work assignments or tasks that will lead to goal attainment, (c) the nature of the supervision to be provided, (d) a statement concerning the work setting, and (e) a statement of the expected number of hours to be worked.

This agreement does three important things for the student. First, it helps ensure that the activities in which the student will be engaged contribute to what should be an important learning experience. Second, it provides the framework for appropriate feedback and evaluation. Third, in the unlikely event a disagreement over work expectations occurs, it serves as an objective source of information that can prove invaluable in resolving the conflict. This document is the key to establishing a good working relationship.

Finally, interns should be careful not to misinterpret a supervisor's casual interpersonal style or the lack of a significant age difference between an intern and a supervisor. Neither of these dynamics signals a disregard for professional standards or organizational hierarchy.

Questions of Authority and Responsibility

Once a field experience agreement has been completed and all parties have agreed to its content, the student and the site supervisor should reread the document carefully to determine what issues of authority and responsibility are created. This is critically important since the nature of the work and the student's relationship with the administrative unit or department create the potential for institutional and personal liability. The following list contains several examples of activities that are commonly found in supervised experiences. Such assignments should not necessarily be avoided, but they do warrant special consideration. Interns should determine if they will be expected to do any of the following:

1. Answering phone calls or other inquiries
2. Handling confidential files or material
3. Attending meetings where sensitive information is shared
4. Distributing information to customers or clients
5. Hiring other student employees
6. Negotiating or signing contracts
7. Operating office or other types of equipment, including computers
8. Supervising others in the department or at events away from the work site
9. Serving as an on-call staff member after normal office hours or on weekends

Each of these activities may carry with it some liability if interns are not appropriately trained or fail to act in a professional manner. This liability may also carry over to the supervisor or employer depending on the line of authority established in the internship agreement and the degree of supervision provided.

Assessing Liability Potential in the Internship

The following exercise may help supervisors and interns identify areas of potential liability and ensure that students are provided with adequate training in those areas. Complete these tasks in order.

Step 1: The intern should ask that the site supervisor complete all of the steps that follow and should schedule a time when the exercise can be discussed.

Step 2: List all the activities identified on the contract in which the intern may be engaged. This may entail identifying some activities that are not listed on the contract but that are associated with accomplishing the tasks listed on the contract or implied in the language of the agreement.

Step 3: For each activity, rate the potential liability using a 3-point scale where 1 = limited liability potential, 2 = moderate liability potential, and 3 = high liability potential.

Step 4: Rank those activities, placing those with the greatest liability risk at the top of a list.

Step 5: For each activity, identify the training or information that should be provided to the intern to ensure adequate precautions have been taken to minimize liability.

Step 6: Amend the intern's work schedule to ensure that time is provided to receive the training or retrieve the information listed in Step 4.

This discussion of authority and responsibility is closely associated with the types of authority that interns might have in the supervised experience setting. Types of authority, therefore, merit some attention.

Types of Authority

Site supervisors and interns alike need to be aware of the kinds and limits of authority that are delegated to interns. From a legal perspective, there are several types of authority. Authority may be express, implied, or apparent (*Brown v. Wichita State University*, Kan. 1975).[2] Express authority may be found in the plain meaning of any written document establishing authority, such as a behavioral contract or job description. For example, an internship contract that states that the student will advise a student group allocates explicit authority to that student to serve in an advisory capacity.

Implied authority emanates from express authority and can be defined as that which is necessary or appropriate for exercising express authority. In the example of the intern who has express authority to serve as an advisor, implied authority allows the intern to sign forms for the group, chaperone group activities, and represent the group's interests to other constituencies. All such activities are assumed to be appropriate for carrying out the duties of a student group advisor.

Students should take care to act based on their express or implied authority. If harm results from the actions of students acting in good faith within the scope of their responsibilities and the authority granted to them, the liability for the injury or breach of contract becomes the responsibility of the supervisor and institution, except in a few extreme circumstances such as violation of a person's civil rights or gross negligence.

Apparent authority is no authority at all. In this instance, a person creates the illusion of authority where none exists. Students involved in field experiences, as well as all other employee groups, should never act with the apparent authority created by a temporary title, the use of letterhead stationery, or the location of their office space. For example, an intern who is serving as an advisor to a student group should not write a letter on letterhead stationary committing resources the group does not have or claim to have reserved space for a student organization when that responsibility belongs to someone else. The liability for harm done by those who rely on the appearance of authority or act without authority may extend to the intern as well as to the supervisor and institution.

Questions of authority and responsibility are especially important if the intern in a supervised experience is authorized to make decisions independently on behalf of the unit or speak on behalf of other administrators. As a general rule, it is unwise to give interns the responsibility or authority to act as a professional practitioner to constituents outside the unit.

Liability Issues

To address the potential liability resulting from a failure to discharge assignments appropriately, it is important to know about confidentiality and student records, defamation, discrimination, negligence, sexual harassment, and circumstances involving mandatory reporting.

Confidentiality and Student Records

Most field placement sites in higher education require interns to work with students and information about students. A federal stature known as the Family Educational Rights and Privacy Act of 1974 (20 U.S.C. § 1232g), popularly known as the Buckley Amendment or FERPA, regulates this information and the resulting student record. The Act and its implementing regulations, 34 C. F. R. Part 99, apply to all public and private educational agencies or institutions that receive federal funds from the US Department of Education or whose students receive such funds under federal loan programs. If a unit and its employees, including interns, engage in compiling or distributing information contained in a student's educational record, they must do so in compliance with this Act. The Act defines what may be included in an educational record and addresses academic, disciplinary, employment, financial, medical, and psychological information. It gives students control of their own records and requires that institutions receive permission from the student before information is released. There are exceptions, of course.

The Act exempts "directory information" for example, but even here, the student should be given the opportunity to make a blanket declaration that this personally identifiable information cannot be released. Directory information includes students' names, addresses, phone numbers, dates of enrollment, and in the case of student athletes, height and weight.

More generally, information that is collected, stored, or transmitted by those acting on behalf of an institution should be handled in a professional and sensitive manner. Regardless of its nature, information should be shared only with those who have a legitimate need to have it. Leaving office records in plain view of those not connected with the office or discussing office matters with friends and other colleagues as idle gossip are ill advised. Such conduct is highly unprofessional and may be deemed unlawful as well.

Issues surrounding confidentiality and student records are critically important if interns are involved in answering phone calls and other inquiries or handle confidential files or attend meetings where sensitive information is discussed. Interns should treat all personally identifiable information obtained in the internship site as *confidential* and should not share it with others outside the site, unless required by law or instructed to do so by an administrator in the organization with express authority.

Defamation

Defamation can be defined as the act of injuring a person's reputation by the distribution of information (Alexander & Alexander, 2011). Defamation through the spoken word is called slander. Defaming someone through a written document is called libel. While defamation suits are not common in the higher education setting, disputes may arise when letters of recommendations, phone references, or performance evaluations are perceived to be negative and harm the person who is the subject of such communication. For a person to be found guilty of defaming another person, four requirements must be met: (a) the statement made is false, (b) the information shared identifies the person who is defamed, (c) the information shared causes at least nominal damage to the person defamed, and (d) the falsehood is attributable to the person sharing the information (Kaplin & Lee, 2013). Allegations of defamation can be avoided by following the best practices and ethical standards discussed later in this chapter.

Discrimination

Those responsible for recruitment, application, interview, and selection processes must exercise great care if they are to avoid liability in the area of employment discrimination. From time to time, students in internships may be involved in these hiring processes. If so, it is important that they know about Title VII of the Civil Rights Act of 1964 (42 U.S.C. § 2000). The statute's basic prohibition is set forth in Section 2000e-2(a), which states the following:

It shall be an unlawful employment practice for an employer to:

(1) fail or refuse to hire or to discharge any individual, or otherwise discriminate against any individual with respect to his compensation, terms, conditions, or privileges of employment, because of such individual's race, color, religion, sex, or national origin; or (2) limit, segregate, or classify his employees or applicants for employment in any way which would deprive or tend to deprive any individual of employment opportunities or otherwise adversely affect his status as an employee, because of such individual's race, color, religion, sex, or national origin.

Other pieces of federal legislation also address discrimination in employment. For example, the Americans With Disabilities Act of 1990 [commonly referred to as ADA] (42 U.S.C. § 12101) and the Rehabilitation Act of 1973 (29 U.S.C. § 794), sometimes referred to as Section 504, forbid employment discrimination against individuals with disabilities. The Age Discrimination Act of 1975 (42 U.S.C. § 6101 et seq.) contains a general prohibition of discrimination against persons age 40 or older in federally funded programs and activities.

Those who hire staff regularly will, more than likely, use office protocols that ensure good hiring practices. These protocols may include guidelines for (a) placing job advertisements, (b) creating application forms, (c) developing interview questions, and (d) conducting reference and background checks. Those who do not hire staff regularly should consult their human resource officers for such guidance and review suggestions offered by Winston and Creamer (1997).

More generally, Title VI of the Civil Rights Act of 1964 (42 U.S.C. § 2000d) and Title IX of the Higher Education Amendments Act (20 U.S.C. § 1681 et seq.)

prohibit discrimination in any education program that receives federal aid. These statutes declare that no person in the United States shall, on the ground of race, color, national origin, or sex, be excluded from participation in, be denied the benefits of, or be subjected to discrimination under any program or activity receiving federal financial aid. These statutes reach beyond employment and cover other important issues such as access and participation by those groups that are protected. Title IX is probably best known because of its application in college athletics. Although it mandates that opportunities for women in sports programs should approximate their presence in the student body, this Act also has serious implications for all educational and workplace environments.

Finally, it is also important to remember that states and individual institutions may also protect additional classifications of individuals through their nondiscrimination clauses. Sexual orientation (including transgender), for example, is identified more and more frequently in such statements. Once states or institutions voluntarily grant such protection, they are obligated to provide it.

Lawsuits stemming from allegations of wrongdoing under these federal and state statutes are litigated with regularity. Hiring staff is a complicated process, and accommodating the disabled in the myriad of educational programs offered on a college campus can pose a serious challenge to even the most experienced administrator. For these reasons, interns and their supervisors should have a thorough understanding of these statutes, especially if interns will be assisting in any employment function or have responsibility for planning events.

Reflection Activity

Here are two different nondiscrimination statements:

1. This university will not tolerate discrimination on the basis of race, color, creed, religion, national origin, sex, gender identity, marital status, veteran or military status, disability, genetic information, age, sexual orientation, status in regard to public assistance, membership or activity in a local commission, or any other characteristic protected by law.
2. We encourage there be an environment of mutual tolerance and respect that is free of hostility toward, discrimination against, or harassment of any person based on race, color, religion, sex, disability, national origin, age, marital or veteran status, or any other status protected by law.

What are the differences in content and spirit of these two statements?

Negligence

Higher education institutions are complex organizations engaged in all kinds of activities that carry some risk. When another person is harmed in some way as a result of these activities, claims of negligence often arise. Examples of these claims might include failing to properly supervise a field trip or classroom activity, allowing the use of equipment without proper training, failing to provide reasonable security of the premises, failing to properly maintain property, or failing to properly warn participants about the risks of an activity or the campus environment.

College and university administrators face a growing array of negligence lawsuits. Although most students have reached the legal age of majority and are responsible for their own behavior, injured students and their parents are increasingly asserting that institutions have a duty of supervision or a duty based on their special relationship with the student. An injured party may prevail in a negligence claim if it can be shown that the institution had a duty of care and that the institution failed to operate within an appropriate standard of care to avoid injury (Hendrickson, 1999). These claims may involve payment from a few hundred dollars to millions of dollars per incident. It is important to remember that interns involved in supervised experiences regardless of their employment status are likely to be viewed as "gratuitous employees," so the liability for their actions may very well be extended to their supervisors and institutions (*Foster v. Board of Trustees of Butler County Community College*, Kan. 1991). For this reason, interns involved in supervised experiences should understand their roles and responsibility for supervising others and should know how to report incidents that involve accidents or unsafe conditions.

The liability surrounding the use of alcoholic beverages is a subject that merits special attention. The vast majority of college students consume alcoholic beverages whether or not they have reached the legal age to do so. Serving alcoholic beverages to students who have not reached 21 years of age or serving those who appear to be intoxicated regardless of age is a violation of state law. The provider of the beverage may, in many states, also be held responsible for the accidents and injuries caused by intoxicated persons (Gehring, Geraci, & McCarthy, 1999). This notion of third-party liability extends to the provider through social host theories (Kaplan & Lee, 2013). Providing, selling, or allowing alcoholic beverages to be consumed at functions that can be connected with the college or university is *always* risky business. The appropriateness of such an activity should be carefully discussed *before* the event. If the decision is made to make alcohol part of the activity, it must be carefully managed and monitored. If interns work with student groups that serve or drink alcohol, they should make sure that all institutional policies and state laws are strictly observed. Should a student attending one of the events be injured, the intern and the institution may be held criminally and/or civilly liable.

Sexual Harassment

Sexual harassment is a relatively new issue in higher education. Its origins are found in Title VII of the Civil Rights Act of 1964 discussed previously in this chapter. While the Act did not provide for a specific cause of action for sexual harassment, the Fifth Circuit Court of Appeals, in *Rogers v. EEOC* (1971), ruled that workplace harassment was prohibited by law. The key to this ruling was that the harassment took the form of racial discrimination. Five years later, in *Williams v. Saxbe* (1976), sexual harassment of a female employee by a supervisor was recognized as a Title VII violation. In 1986, the Supreme Court embraced this concept in its landmark case, *Meritor Savings Bank v. Vinson*, and reaffirmed its ban on gender-based harassment in *Harris v. Forklift Systems* (1993).

In the higher education environment, the concept of sexual harassment has been extended to the classroom and the relationship between professors and their students. Even more recently, courts have ruled same-sex sexual harassment (*Nogueras v. University of Puerto Rico*, 1995) and student-to-student harassment (*Davis v. Monroe County Board of Education*, 1999) were covered by federal nondiscrimination statutes.

Sexual harassment is defined as "unwelcomed sexual advances, requests for sexual favors or other verbal or physical conduct of a sexual nature" (29 C.F.R. §1604.11a). Sexual harassment can take one of two forms: quid pro quo sexual harassment and hostile work environment sexual harassment.

Quid pro quo sexual harassment is the coercion of another into performing an unwelcomed sexual act as a part of a bargain to obtain favors or avoid punitive actions. In the higher education setting, these favors or punitive actions might include appointments, promotions, higher wages or salaries, or grades.

Hostile work environment harassment occurs when individuals, because of their gender, experience a work environment "permeated with discriminatory intimidating, ridicule, and insult which are sufficiently severe or pervasive to alter the conditions of employment and create an abusive working environment" (29 C.F.R. §1604.11a). Both forms of sexual harassment can be devastating.

Almost all colleges and universities in the country have formal statements that define sexual harassment. Harassment can include offensive remarks about a person's sex. For example, it is illegal to harass a woman by making offensive comments about women in general (US Equal Opportunity Commission, n.d.). Interns should become familiar with their institution's and the internship-hosting institution's (if different) definitions and policies about sexual harassment.

Circumstances Requiring Reporting

Because of several recent incidents involving sexual harassment and sexual violence in educational settings, the Office of Civil Rights (OCR) has provided additional guidance on how this form of discrimination must be addressed (see US Department of Education, April 4, 2011). In addition to provisions on policy development, implementation, and notification, the OCR reemphasized the obligation for all "campus security authorities" to report incidents of sexual harassment and violence to the institution's Title IX coordinator. While most graduate student interns are not likely to be designated as such, those who advise student organizations or monitor campus facilities may be designated as campus security authorities (US Department of Education, 2011). Interns who have questions about their status in this regard should discuss their concerns with their supervisors as soon as possible.

Interns who find themselves in new office surroundings should be careful about entering into inappropriate office banter or passing along off-color humor to colleagues. These seemingly harmless activities could add to or help create a work environment that others find insulting and harassing. Interns who witness incidents of more serious sexual harassment or violence or who learn of incidents indirectly should contact their site supervisors immediately.

Liability Management

Interns and their supervisors have an obligation to protect themselves and their institutions from the legal liability that may result from the vast array of activities that may be connected with supervised experiences. Using a three-step liability management process can help determine and reduce one's exposure to lawsuits: (a) determine the potential for harm, (b) determine the cost of the potential lawsuit, and (c) determine a liability-reduction strategy.

Determine the Potential for Harm

First, individuals should examine their administrative decisions, activities, and plans for their *potential for harm to others*. A particular decision may have no potential, some potential, or a severe potential for harm. An example may serve to illustrate the point.

Making a request that an office worker rearrange a stock room of routine office supplies consisting of paper products, pens, and paper clips carries minimal potential for harm. The materials are lightweight, easy to handle, and pose no real danger in and of themselves. Asking the same office worker to unload and uncrate a shipment of heavy office equipment without the proper safety equipment and some instruction on how to lift heavy objects, on the other hand, carries a greater potential for harm. In the second instance, there is a much greater potential for personal injury, such as back strain or hand or foot injuries, if a crate is dropped.

Determining the potential for harm is not an exact science, but it is a critical first step in managing the liability connected with administrative decisions, activities, or plans. Use all of the data available in the workplace and a healthy dose of common sense to develop these calculations.

Determine the Cost of the Potential Lawsuit

The second step in this process is to determine the approximate cost of the lawsuit if one were to result from one's actions. The point of the exercise is not to determine the exact cost of the legal action but to place a reasonable dollar value on a negative outcome. If an institution employs legal counsel as part of a permanent staff, there may be no additional cost to mounting a legal defense since the attorney is already on staff. If legal counsel must be retained before the institution can defend itself, these costs could be considerable. Recent court decisions and awards made by juries in similar kinds of cases may serve as helpful guides to estimate the cost of an adverse ruling. In the case of workplace injuries, human resource officers can probably provide cost estimates for workman's compensation claims and lost productivity if an employee is absent from work.

Determine a Liability-Reduction Strategy

Once these two estimates are obtained, they can be plotted on the matrix shown in Figure 5.1. This visual aid graphically illustrates how much risk is involved in any administrative decision, action, or plan. Where potential for harm is low and the cost of a potential lawsuit is low (quadrant 1), administrators can assume it is safe to act. In all other quadrants, higher levels of professional judgment must be exercised.

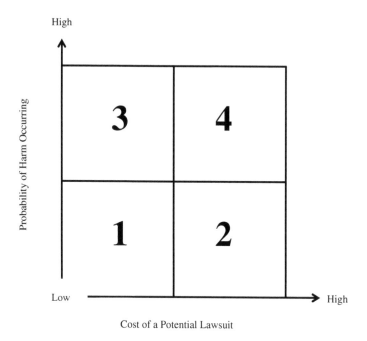

Figure 5.1 Management liability matrix.

If an administrative action falls into quadrant 4 (that is, high potential for harm and high cost of the potential lawsuit), the most prudent course of action may be to avoid the activity altogether; avoiding is a legitimate liability management strategy. But even in this case, administrators, in some instances, may want to make the decision to plan the activity. If they choose to go forward, they can reduce exposure to their liability by (a) *transferring* responsibility for the risk, (b) *insuring* themselves against the risk, or (c) *managing* the risk. These strategies may be used alone or in combination with one another. There are times, however, that an institution may elect to proceed with an activity in quadrant 4 if the potential educational benefits are sufficiently high (Winston & Saunders, 1998).

Another example may serve to illustrate how this works. Suppose representatives from the senior class approach the administration and request to hold a senior party between the last day of exams and graduation. They want to hold the event on campus and serve alcoholic beverages. While most of the seniors will be of legal age to consume alcohol, their dates and some family members may not be of age. What could be done to manage the potential liability created by such an event?

Working with representative of the senior class, administrators could plan to *transfer* some of the liability for serving beverage alcohol by contracting with a catering service. The caterer would have to be licensed to sell beer, wine, and mixed beverages and be trained to serve responsibly. Administrators and the senior class would not purchase or distribute the beverage. The event sponsors could also contract with off-duty police officers to enforce state laws and thus *transfer* the liability connected with enforcement issues.

In addition, sponsors could *manage* the event so as to reduce the potential for accidents by establishing certain ground rules for the event. They could require that colored wrist bans be worn by event participants so that age could be easily determined, set a maximum drink limit per person, restrict the size of the drink to be served, or limit the time period in which beverages will be served.

Finally, the institution and senior class could obtain special event liability insurance that would cover the costs associated with lawsuits that may result if accidents or injuries occur. Such a policy would *insure* the sponsors from liability. Once these strategies are put in place, the potential for harm and the cost of any potential lawsuit should be recalculated. If the risks have been sufficiently reduced, the event could be held.

Students interested in learning more about risk reduction strategies should read *Reducing Administrative Liability in Higher Education* by Janosik and Andrews (1985) and *Anticipating Legal Issues in Higher Education* by Janosik (2005).

Compensation Issues

The concept of an apprenticeship serving as a means of training skilled workers dates to the Middle Ages (Burke & Carton, 2013). Such activities, now called internships or practica, can be an effective way for students to gain skills necessary for professional success. Students assigned to such positions can be paid or unpaid. With the recent passage of the Patient Protection and Affordable Care Act, Pub. L. No. 111–148, popularly known as the Affordable Care Act, employers need to exercise great care in determining the status of their interns when they are compensated for the work performed. While a detailed discussion of the legal issues connected with this new law is well beyond the scope of this text, it worthwhile to mention that student interns may be required to carefully document the number of hours they work. Employers are most likely to insist that a student intern work less than an average of 30 hours per week, regardless of the student's interest or desire. The reason for this careful documentation is that employers with at least 50 employees must provide some form of health care benefits to their full-time employees (i.e., persons who work an average of 30 hours per week). Many human resource officers are aware of the fines involved for violating the provisions of this Act and anticipate heightened enforcement in the short term. Interns should be clear about their work schedule and how they are to record the number of hours worked. Adhering to these procedures is crucially important.

Professional Standards and Ethics

The first section of this chapter has focused on the law, the implications for failing to adhere to certain federal statutes, and the liability that may result from that failure. While the law provides a good framework for professional behavior, it, is not, by itself, complete. Even though the law and its standards provide appropriate counsel, everything that is legal is not always ethical. Hate speech is an example that illustrates this principle. Despite the fact that saying hateful things that cause individuals to feel uncomfortable might be protected by the First Amendment of the US Constitution, such behavior would not be condoned by most professional standards or ethics codes. Consequently, the remainder of this chapter is devoted to professional standards and ethics.

Reaching agreement on a common set of professional or ethical standards is not as easy as it may appear, especially for a profession that is as diverse as higher education and student affairs administration. A special ethics taskforce for the National Association of Student Personnel Administrators recently wrote,

> [its] attempt to identify themes and consistencies between NASPA's professional code of ethics and the codes of other Student Affairs related professional organizations . . . did not yield useful ethical guidelines that would serve the diverse members of our organization across positions, experiences, and worldviews equally well.
>
> (NASPA Ethics Statement, July 2012, p. 1)

Despite this assertion, most professional associations promote ethical behavior (or standards) through their various codes, principles, or statements. Three such codes are provided in the appendices of this book. The National Association of Student Personnel Administrators' (NASPA) Ethical Professional Practice can be found in Appendix 6 and the American College Personnel Association's (ACPA) Statement of Ethical Principles and Standards (last revised in 2006) can be found in Appendix 7. Both of these organizations serve large numbers of professionals in the field of higher education administration and student development. The third document was developed by the Council for the Advancement of Standards (CAS), a group founded to implement several profession-wide initiatives, with emphasis on the development and promulgation of professional standards. Its Statement of Shared Ethical Principles (1997) was written specifically to acknowledge the diversity in the profession, while emphasizing an over-arching common commitment to certain ethical principles. It can be found in Appendix 8.

The NASPA statement provided in Appendix 6 is a good general review of the expectations for ethical behavior primarily from an institutional perspective. It addresses three levels of ethical conduct: basic, intermediate, and advanced. ACPA's statement (2006), on the other hand, is more complex and is more focused on the conduct of individual practitioners. It includes a preamble, a mechanism for enforcement, a section on general ethical principles, and a very detailed section on ethical standards. Finally, the CAS statement (1997), "focuses on seven basic principles that form the foundation for CAS member association codes: autonomy, non-malfeasance, beneficence, justice, fidelity, veracity, and affiliation" (p. 1). Each is worth reading and discussing as part of an intern's orientation to a new supervised experience.

Other professional associations have developed their own ethical statements around their particular functional area. The Association of College and University Housing Officers-International (ACUHO-I), for example, has its own statement that endorses the ACPA statement and adds standards specific to housing and residence life professionals. The Association for Student Conduct Administration (formally known as the Association for Student Judicial Affairs) last revised its code in 1993. It includes 14 sections describing ethical and professional conduct for those involved in student discipline. As a final example, the National Orientation Directors Association (NODA) developed its statement of ethical standards that includes separate sections for professionals and student interns. It also references ACPA's Statement of Ethical Principles and Standards. All of these documents can serve as valuable resources for the practitioner.

Once students are placed at a site, they should ask about any ethical statements or principles that may exist for the institution, student affairs division, or functional area. Individual institutions and departments may also develop policies that govern professional behavior. These should be reviewed thoroughly at an early stage in the supervised experience. Such statements serve as excellent guides and highlight important professional issues that should be discussed with the site supervisor.

Ethical Principles

Even though codes and lists of standards can be helpful, no standards statement can cover all situations. Consideration of certain ethical principles affords one a helpful degree of flexibility while maintaining consistency. To accommodate the ambiguity found in some of these situations, one group of professionals suggests practitioners ask themselves three questions to help them address their decision-making process:

1. What does the greater good, benevolence, or compassion look like in this situation?
2. What thoughts, ideas, behaviors, and relationships will be expanded or reduced from what is created by my decision?
3. Does the decision respect my individual values and the integrity of all people being affected by it? (NASPA, July 2012, p. 3)

These questions coupled with a list of principles frequently cited in the ethics literature developed by Kitchener (1985) can serve as a useful framework to address ethical dilemmas. This list suggests professionals should (a) respect autonomy, (b) do no harm, (c) benefit others, (d) be just, and (e) be faithful.

Respecting autonomy means allowing others to decide how they live their own lives so long as their actions do not interfere with the rights and welfare of others. In the context of student development, respecting autonomy allows students the freedom to make their own mistakes and learn from them. For example, the intern who is serving as a group advisor might learn that the group's president has decided to invite a certain speaker to address the group without seeking input from the group's membership before issuing the invitation. The advisor thinks this is ill advised and will prompt reactions from group members that could lead to the president's removal from office, either virtually or literally. However, since it is within the president's purview to invite speakers to the group's meetings, and the president's decision does not interfere with the rights or welfare of the group, the advisor may elect not to interfere and allow the president learn from this experience.

Doing no harm means that individuals have an obligation to avoid behavior that would cause physical or psychological injuries to others. An intern working with new students in an orientation program, for example, should avoid making blanket statements about certain types of students (e.g., those who are very bright or those who participate in athletics). There may be students in the audience who are members of such groups who would be embarrassed or feel demeaned by the comments.

Acting to benefit others means that individuals should act in good faith with one another. Actions that are helpful do not always have to be pleasant. For example, the intern who works in a student conduct office may be required to inform students they have violated campus policy and are to be sanctioned. Explaining this in a professional manner and discussing the learning that can accrue from such sanctions models the behaviors the intern hopes to see in the students who are in violation of the code.

Being just means being fair or treating those with whom we come in contact equally. This does not mean that there will always be an equal outcome, but it does mean that everyone will be judged on the same criteria. Consider interns who work with students in the residence halls. One group of residents may be making an excessive amount of noise by playing rap music on a boom box while another group of students may be making excessive noise by playing gospel music on their stereo. While the intern's taste may favor one type of music over the other, both groups are making excessive noise and need to be dealt with accordingly.

Being faithful means that professionals keep their promises, tell the truth, and are loyal to their colleagues and institutions. This may seem to be a straightforward assumption. If the intern says he or she will have the report on hazing in the fraternity and sorority system completed on a certain date, that report should be submitted. But what if the intern learns in the process of gathering data for the report that publishing what really goes on in Greek chapters will result in a lot of negative press for the institution, particularly for the intern's supervisor who advises the Greek system on campus? Dilemmas such as this are more frequent than might be expected and aspiring practitioners need to hone their values and ethics so they are prepared to cope with the ambiguities of professional practice.

Interns, and professionals as well, can benefit from the following suggestions with respect to ethical dilemmas and professional practice:

1. Always examine the legal requirements *and* ethical implications surrounding an action.
2. Consult a mentor or trusted colleague who has no stake in the situation when questions or uncertainty arises.
3. Handle ethical concerns quickly with those most directly involved.
4. Discuss ethics and standards regularly as part of your professional routine.

Being Practical About Ethics

Applying these ethical principles to daily life can be difficult. As noted earlier, conflicts among ethical principles and ethical standards occur frequently. To continue with the hate speech example, allowing students to engage in hate speech may satisfy the respect autonomy principle but would violate the do no harm principle. When choices between principles must be made, one ought to be able to articulate a clear rationale for doing so. In allowing hate speech to occur on campus, courts often point to the traditional value of academic freedom held by public higher education, for example. This value suggests that the free exchange of ideas is critical to the educational process even when these views might be unpopular or repugnant to some. Finding a balance in one's ethical practice is not easy. Another common ethical difficulty involves the dual relationship.

Dual Relationships: A Special Case

Before concluding this chapter on legal and ethical issues, we want to address an often-encountered workplace dilemma known as the dual relationship. In the workplace, a dual relationship exists when two individuals assume additional roles beyond that of supervisor–supervisee. Such relationships may not be illegal but are unethical in almost every case. Such relationships have the potential to do great harm and at the very least create negative or awkward workplace dynamic. Examples of dual relationships are (a) an employee who views a supervisor as a confidant or counselor with respect to matters that are not work related, (b) a supervisor who develops an extremely close personal relationship with a subordinate, or (c) a graduate hall director who becomes sexually intimate with a resident. When supervisors or those in positions of authority become involved in additional roles such as counselor, best friend, or lover, the ability to remain objective about job performance or to remain impartial becomes difficult if not impossible. Most ethical standards prohibit such relationships, and many employers have personnel policies that prohibit these relationships as well.

Many professionals dismiss this concern about dual relationships, thinking that they can remain unbiased and objective. Many professionals think that they can compartmentalize their relationships and eliminate any harm to the other party. Graduate assistants, in particular, are prone to adopt such attitudes. They might argue, "If I can't date undergraduates, there would be no one to date." New professionals in student affairs might also share this feeling, especially when living in small college towns where there may be few professionals of similar age or few young adults who do not work for the institution. But such attitudes fail to take the perceptions of others into consideration. In many instances it might be just as debilitating and just as disruptive to create the appearance of unethical behavior as it would to engage in unethical behavior.

Reflective Activity

Consider the following example:

An associate director of student activities and a coordinator of leadership development have worked in the same office for 3 years. They share common interests and hobbies. They work together on assignments, share office space, and share clerical support staff. The department operates as a team and socializes regularly outside the office. The two become good friends. They do not consider themselves a couple, but they do spend lots of time together outside the office.

The current assistant director of student activities leaves midyear, and two inside candidates apply for the interim position. The coordinator who shares office space with the associate director is exceptionally well qualified and the much better qualified of the two inside candidates. The director and associate director make the decision to promote the coordinator to the interim position. Shortly after the announcement is made, anonymous flyers are placed in the staff's office mailboxes that reads "Qualifications for Promotion in Student Activities.—Have Sex with the Associate Director." A similar statement that identifies the office and the individuals involved is also posted on an untraceable Facebook site.

Questions

1. Did the associate director and coordinator do anything unethical?
2. What could the director, associate director, or coordinator have done to anticipate this difficulty?
3. Would the ethical guides found in the appendices have helped avoid this situation? If so, how?
4. Now that some staff members have read the flyers, what should the director, associate director, and coordinator do now?

Office romances are common in student affairs just as they are in other professions. They offer employees some of the most difficult ethical challenges one can face.

Other Sensitive Human Resource Issues

Other personnel decisions such as hiring and firing staff can create various serious ethical dilemmas.

Reflective Activity

Imagine the following circumstance:

You, as a department intern, are supervising a student worker. The student has been chronically late for work, has made long distance and personal phone calls almost daily, and has taken office supplies for her personal use. You have witnessed and documented all of these behaviors.

After you consulted with your site supervisor, your site supervisor fires the student worker.

Several days have passed, and you hear from a fellow intern that he is considering hiring the same student for another part-time student position in a different office. Your colleague makes the following statement, "This student seems highly motivated, very personable. My only concern is that she has absolutely no work experience, so I cannot get a job reference from anyone. I think I am going to go ahead and take a chance on her."

Identify the legal and ethical issues connected with this dilemma. Review the Kitchener principles outlined in this chapter. Do they help focus your understanding of the issues associated with this case study?

What would you do in this circumstance?

Conclusions

Supervised experiences are an important part of any professional preparation program. They are designed to complement and enhance classroom learning, aid in the transition from theory to practice, and give the student a first-hand look at the world of work. In most instances, students will be expected to become fully participating members of the staff with all of the responsibilities attached thereto. Depending on the assignment, some of these responsibilities carry a degree of legal liability and all of them carry the expectation that the student will behave in a professional and ethical manner.

This chapter is designed to highlight the legal and ethical issues connected with supervised experiences. Students who understand these concepts, ask questions, and act on the knowledge gained through their inquiry will ensure their success.

Reflection Activity

Interns should give some time and thought to these issues by completing the following tasks:

1. Interns should ask their supervisors to identify the top three legal issues that have the greatest potential for lawsuits and discuss how the department is managing those legal risks.
2. Interns who are unfamiliar with the litigation process should attend a civil trial in the nearest municipal court.
3. Interns should ask to see the department's procedures for hiring and the institution's policy statement on affirmative action. Then, discuss how they complement one another.
4. Interns should ask for a copy of the institution's sexual harassment policy and discuss how it was developed. Do its provisions exceed state or federal law?
5. Interns should ask their site supervisors to discuss the most difficult ethical situation they have experienced and talk about how it was resolved.

Notes

1. Nothing is this chapter should be construed as legal advice. When legal issues arise, one should always seek the counsel of a competent attorney.
2. For information about how to read and understand legal citations, see Gehring (2001).

References

29 CFR § 1604.11a. Title 29: Labor Part 1604–Guidelines on Discrimination Because of Sex. Retrieved from www.ecfr.gov/cgi-bin/text-idx?SID=68669f89dfba342bfd9445d1ab3f59d1&node=29:4.1.4.1.5.0.21.11&rgn=div8

Age Discrimination Act of 1975, 42 U.S.C. § 6101 et seq.

Alexander, K. W., & Alexander, K. (2011). *Higher education law: Policy and perspectives.* New York, NY: Routledge.

American College Personnel Association (ACPA). (2006). *Statement of ethical principles and standards.* Retrieved from www.myacpa.org/au/documents/EthicsStatement.pdf

Americans With Disabilities Act of 1990, 42 U.S.C. § 12101.

Brown v. Wichita State University, 540 P.2d 66 (Kan. 1975).

Burke, D., & Carton, R. (2013). The pedagogical, legal, and ethical implications of unpaid internships. *Journal of Legal Studies Education, 30*(1), 99–130.

Council for the Advancement of Standards (CAS). (1997). *Statement of shared ethical principles.* Washington, DC: Author.

Davis v. Monroe County Board of Education, 526 U.S. 629, 120 F.3d 1390 (1999).

Family Educational Rights and Privacy Act, 20 U.S.C. § 1232g (1974).

Foster v. Board of Trustees of Butler County Community College, 771 F. Supp. 1122 (D. Kan. 1991).

Gehring, D. D. (2001). An introduction to legal research. In R. B. Winston, Jr., D. G. Creamer, T. K. Miller, & Associates, *The professional student affairs administrator: Educator, leader, and manager* (pp. 415–419). Philadelphia, PA: Brunner-Routledge.

Gehring, D. D., Geraci, C. P., & McCarthy, T. (1999). *Alcohol on campus: A compendium of the law and guide to campus policy* (Rev.). Asheville, NC: College Administration.

Harris v. Forklift Systems, Inc., 510 U.S. 17 (1993).

Hendrickson, R. M. (1999). *The colleges, their constituencies, and the courts* (2nd ed.). Dayton, OH: Education Law Association.

Janosik, S. M. (2005). Anticipating legal issues in higher education, *NASPA Journal, 42*(4), 401–414.

Janosik, S. M., & Andrews, L. D. (1985). Reducing institutional and individual liability in higher education. *NASPA Journal, 22*(3), 2–9.

Kaplin, W. A., & Lee, B. A. (2013). *The law of higher education* (5th ed.). San Francisco, CA: Jossey-Bass.

Kitchener, K. S. (1985). Ethical principles and ethical decisions in student affairs. In H. J. Canon & R. D. Brown (Eds.), *Applied ethics in student services.* New Directions for Student Services, No. 30. San Francisco, CA: Jossey-Bass.

Meritor Savings Bank v. Vinson, 477 U.S. 57 (1986).

NASPA (1990). *Ethical professional practice.* Retrieved from www.naspa.org/about/student-affairs/ethical-professional-practice

NASPA (2012, July). *NASPA ethics statement.* Unpublished report. Washington, DC.

Nogueras v. University of Puerto Rico, 890 F. Supp. 60 (1995).

Patient Protection and Affordable Care Act, Pub. L. No. 111–148 (2010).

Rehabilitation Act of 1973, 29 U.S.C. § 794.

Rogers v. EEOC, 454 F.2d 234 (5th Cir. 1971).

Title VI of the Civil Rights Act of 1964, 42 U.S.C. § 2000d.

Title VII of the Civil Rights Act of 1964, 42 U.S.C. § 2000.

Title IX of the Higher Education Amendments Act, 20 U.S.C. § 1681 et seq. (1972).

US Department of Education, Office of Civil Rights. (2011, April 4). *Dear colleague letter.* Washington, DC: Author.

US Department of Education, Office of Postsecondary Education. (2011). *The handbook for campus safety and security reporting.* Washington, DC: Author.

US Equal Employment Opportunity Commission (n.d.). Sexual Harassment, para. 2. Retrieved from www.eeoc.gov/laws/types/sexual_harassment.cfm

Williams v. Saxbe, 413 F. Supp. 654 (D.D.C. 1976).

Winston, R. B., Jr., & Creamer, D. G. (1997). *Improving staffing practices in student affairs.* San Francisco, CA: Jossey-Bass.

Winston, R. B., Jr., & Saunders, S. A. (1998). Professional ethics in a risky world. In D. L. Cooper & J. M. Lancaster (Eds.), *Beyond law and policy: Reaffirming the role of student affairs* (pp. 77–94). New Directions for Student Services, No. 82. San Francisco, CA: Jossey-Bass.

6   Understanding Organizational Contexts

The information we have provided in this volume so far has primarily focused on the individual: what aspiring professionals can learn from an internship, how to design a meaningful practicum, how to deal with supervisors, and how policies and laws influence the intern's experience. All internships take place in an organizational context, however, and beginning student affairs administrators should recognize the role that context plays in professional practice.

The organization is the nucleus of this chapter. To start, it is essential to understand that the term *organization* does not have a static meaning. An organization may be a unit within a department (e.g., the office of clubs and organizations within the Department of Student Activities, the criminology track within a Department of Sociology), a department (e.g., Multicultural Affairs, History), a collection of departments (e.g., a Division of Student Affairs, a College of Arts and Sciences), an entire institution or university, a university system (e.g., the State University of New York), a group of institutions (e.g., liberal arts colleges in the United States), or even the entire system of higher education. In short, we have to define what we mean by the term organization each time we want to examine what may be happening in the work setting.

The many perspectives or frames through which to view them further complicate the fluid nature of organizations. Scholars have written volumes on organizational theory. Some offer typologies of organization theories *writ large* (e.g., Bolman & Deal, 2008; Morgan, 2006) while others have concentrated on higher education (e.g., Bergquist & Pawlak, 2008). Indeed, there are far more organizational frames than we can reasonably address in a single chapter. Instead, we start by briefly describing three of the most common lenses through which to view organizations: the structural, the human resource, and the biological. The intent is to demonstrate how most people tend to use one or two dominant perspectives when trying to understand what is going on around them. Expanding one's repertoire of organizational perspectives increases the range of responses one can take in any given situation. The remainder of the chapter is devoted to two additional perspectives that we believe are particularly useful to student affairs professionals: the political and the cultural. For each of these latter two frames we include a discussion of different forms of diversity that may inform professional practice.

Common Organizational Lenses

Aspiring student affairs professionals undertake a practicum or internship to learn more about a specific functional area such as career services or student conduct. In most cases, they also want to learn more about how the selected office operates. Organizational theories help professionals make sense of their work settings. Although there are numerous theories that practitioners can use, most people tend to rely on two or three theories, and one of those dominates their thinking. For many administrators, that dominant theory is structuralism (Bolman & Deal, 2008) or the bureaucratic frame (Morgan, 2006).

Structuralism focuses on organizational goals and how work is distributed and synchronized to achieve those goals (Martinez-Leon & Martinez-Garcia, 2011). In general, structuralists assume that organizations exist to achieve specified goals and that the manner in which they operate promotes or inhibits the achievement of those goals. Key operational components include differentiation (the assignment of tasks to different individuals) and integration (how work across individuals is coordinated) (Bolman & Deal, 2008). Organizational charts that identify job titles and job descriptions that spell out responsibilities are examples of work differentiation. Having policies and procedures that all employees follow and holding regular staff meetings are typical manifestations of how work is coordinated. Colleges and universities are rife with examples of structuralism. Indeed, as humans we seek to categorize and make sense of our work; hence, we need the order that structuralism can provide (Gebauer, Putz, Fischer, & Fleisch, 2009).

As with all organizational theories, however, there are inherent limitations to structuralism (Legerer, Pfeiffer, Schneider, & Wagner, 2009). In seeking to make sense of the work setting through the way work is managed, for example, it is easy to overlook the human element in the organization. People do not always fulfill all their job duties or comply with policies and procedures (Walczak, 2005). When incidents occur and organizational operations are disrupted, the typical response from the structuralist is to assume the current structure is not working and that a reorganization of the unit is warranted (Bolman & Deal, 2008; Morgan, 2006) when, in fact, the disruption might be addressed by retraining the errant staff member. Administrators who operate solely from the structural or bureaucratic frame may miss problems that lie outside the differentiation and integration of work.

Indeed, the emphasis on the organization that structuralism imposes prompted the development of a second commonly used theory, the human resource perspective (Bolman & Deal, 2008). In this framework, it is the people, not that organization, that matter. Administrators who operate from the human resource perspective assume that when there is a good fit between individuals and the organization, both thrive. Conversely, when the fit is bad, both organizational members and the organization itself suffer (Bolman & Deal, 2008; Jacobs & Park, 2009). Student affairs professionals, trained in developmental theory and dedicated to promoting growth among students, often embrace the human resource perspective when trying to understand their workplace.

As with emphasizing the structural lens, focusing solely on people also limits an administrator's understanding of the workplace. For example, by keying in only on the people, professionals can miss structural issues that may be impeding organizational success (Burns & Otte, 1999). Likewise, it is possible that people get along with one another but are not as productive as they might be. This sort of incomplete picture of the organization can hamper administrative efforts to improve performance (Guest, 2011).

In fact, it is group performance that forms the nexus of the third commonly used organizational lens among student affairs professionals, the biological perspective (Morgan, 2006). There are actually several lenses subsumed under the biological label, all of which view organizations in relationship to their environment (Dooley, Kevin, Douglas, & Dietz, 2013). There are two that many student affairs professionals embrace, however. The population ecology lens assumes that the fittest will survive. Organizations compete for resources from the environment, and those that secure the most resources thrive (Heine & Rindfleisch, 2013). Remember that the definition of organization is fluid. To illustrate population ecology one need only think about the typical budget allocation process used by most student activities offices. Clubs and organizations typically are required to prepare a budget proposal that is presented to a board (often comprised of student government officials). Those organizations are competing for a limited number of student activity dollars and those that secure the greatest funding thrive while those awarded fewer dollars than requested must adapt. Regrettably, if practitioners only view organizations through the population ecology lens, they overlook the fact that at times, it is advantageous for organizations to collaborate.

In the alternative biological lens, organizational ecology, groups cooperate with one another to influence the environment they share (Morgan, 2006). Said another way, there is strength in numbers, and at times the power of the collective allows organizations to shape, rather than be shaped by, the environment (Reydon & Scholz, 2009). For example, when university presidents from public institutions across a state collectively lobby state legislators for more autonomy, they are collaborating and attempting to influence the regulatory environment for the higher education enterprise in their state. Likewise, fraternities and sororities typically compete with one another in a variety of activities such as recruiting members or social events. However Panhellenic and Interfraternity Councils exist on most campuses. These cooperatives act on behalf of the Greek community when they wish to influence the environment (e.g., when administrators attempt to impose regulations on social gatherings). Collaboration, however, has its limits, and those who look at their workplace only through the organizational ecology lens limit their ability to act in other ways when circumstances so dictate.

Student affairs professionals commonly use these three organizational lenses—the structural, the human resource, and the biological—to make sense of their workplace. Each lens offers an appealing, yet incomplete picture of the organization. The structuralist who looks only at the roles employees fulfill to achieve the organizational goals risks overlooking the satisfaction of those same employees. The professional whose only concern is whether employees are fulfilled may fail to notice organizational dysfunction. Operating solely from the perspective of competition or collaboration ignores the importance of both structure and people in achieving group goals.

On the other hand, the practitioner who can view the workplace through all these lenses will have a more complete picture and the flexibility to address problems in multidimensional and creative ways. The practicum setting is an ideal opportunity for aspiring student affairs professionals to (a) identify the organizational perspective they tend to use most frequently, (b) intentionally expand their repertoire of perspectives, and (c) develop tools to address organizational issues from multiple perspectives.

Reflection Activity

Assume you are an intern in the Career Services Office on the campus of a midsized university that offers a wide array of bachelor's and master's degrees but no doctorates. On your first day, your supervisor plans to orient you and provide an overview of the office and its work. There are three ways the supervisor may approach this task. Read each option and then think about the questions posed after all three.

Option A: Your supervisor starts by providing you the mission statement for the office and explains that the statement explains the goals for the office. Then she gives you an organizational chart for the Career Services Department and explains how the different units, such as Employer Relations, Placement Services, and Cooperative Education, work together to provide students with a broad range of services. Next, she gives you an organizational chart for the Division of Student Affairs and explains the role the Career Services Office plays within the division. She takes you on a tour of the office to show you where different activities take place. As you tour, she introduces you to people, giving you their names and then explaining what jobs they hold within the Office. Finally, she reviews with you what responsibilities you will assume as an intern and how you will be supervised and evaluated over the course of your internship.

Option B: You are scheduled to report to your internship Monday morning. On the Wednesday before your first day, your supervisor contacts you and invites you to be his guest for breakfast on Monday before you go to the office. He wants to get to know you a bit and also wants you to have an opportunity to get to know him. You agree and meet for breakfast, during which he tells you about his background and how he prefers to work with his staff. He asks you about how you came to be in your graduate program and what your professional aspirations are. After breakfast, he accompanies you to the office and starts by walking around and introducing you to the other staff. He introduces you by name to each person and goes on to tell you how long that person has worked at the university and a bit about him or her personally. For example, in introducing you to Miguel, your supervisor explains that Miguel is a graduate of the university who has been with Career Services for six years and that Miguel's wife, Emilia, also works on campus in the Office of Student Activities. After he has introduced you to everyone, your supervisor show you your workspace and then takes you to the supply room. He tells you to take the rest of the morning to take any supplies you think you will need and to set up your office so that you are comfortable in that workspace. If you get set up before noon, he encourages you to spend the rest of the morning walking around and talking with staff about Career Services or observing what others are doing. He tells you he will meet with you again that afternoon to see how your first day went.

Option C: Your supervisor sets up a time to meet with you on the morning of the first day of your internship. She starts the meeting by talking about the importance of the Career Services Office to the larger university's mission, telling you she wants you to understand the context of the Career Service Office environment. High school enrollments in your state are dwindling, she explains, so it is increasingly difficult to admit the 2,500 students in an entering class that guarantees that the university will get its full funding from the state. She says that one of the major marketing tools the university is using to recruit students is the placement rates for graduates. During the past 5 years, 82% of graduates have been employed in full-time jobs or enrolled as full-time graduate students within 6 months of completing their degrees. The university uses these data to recruit students and convince them (and their parents) that graduates will succeed. She also talks about the kinds of programs that are offered through the Career Services Office and points out how some of those programs differ from the programs offered by counterparts at other institutions in the state. She concludes by telling you that she would like you to attend the state conference of career services professionals that will take place next month so that you can gain a better sense of how the functional arena operates in general and what is unique about the Career Services Office at your institution.

Reflection Questions

1.   Which of the three options would you prefer if you were the intern?
2.   Why did you select that option?
3.   What does your selection tell you about the lens you might use to view organizations?
4.   What are the limitations to the option you selected? That is, what would you *not* learn about the organization based on the way the orientation was handled?

The odds are that you like select elements of each of the three options, but that one resonated with you more than the other two. Option A represented a structural approach, Option B a human resource approach, and Option C a biological approach to the orientation. If you found one the most comfortable, that is likely your preferred or dominant lens through which you understand organizations. By looking at the organization through different lenses, however, you may gain a richer understanding of the operation that, in turn, will enable you to address organizational issues from a broader perspective.

The Political Perspective

Beyond the three organizational perspectives commonly used by entering student affairs professionals, there are two other frames that we believe are quite useful for practitioners. The first is the political perspective (Bolman & Deal, 2008; Morgan, 2006). This frame is premised on two basic concepts. The first is that conflict in organizations is not only inevitable, it is necessary (Kola, 2013). For many student affairs administrators, this is an anathema. We are powerfully socialized to promote growth and development, not conflict. Yet there are parallels to the notion of organizational conflict in developmental theory. For example, many theorists argue that dissonance is the catalyst to cognitive development (e.g., Kohlberg, 1969; Perry, 1970). That is, something must occur that cannot be addressed through the learner's current cognitive frame, and that conflict must be resolved. Resolving the conflict typically leads to developmental growth. In the same sense, in the political frame, conflict promotes organizational growth and change. If administrators come to appreciate the role that conflict plays in organizations, they may be better able to use conflict in constructive ways.

The political perspective is grounded in the notion that most important decisions in organizations revolve around the allocation of resources (Bolman & Deal, 2008; Ferris & Treadway, 2012) and that resources are always scarce and must be apportioned (Andrews & Kacmar, 2001). It is essential to note that the term *resources* is broadly defined and goes well beyond fiscal resources. For example, on many campuses office space is scarce. For faculty, their most precious resource is time (Lawrence & Ott, 2013), and the way they allocate their time dictates their productivity. In units such as residence life where there are typically many entry-level professionals and far fewer midlevel managers, access to supervision and mentoring may be considered a scarce resource (Harris & Rosen, 2009). Scarce resources, then, take many forms.

To compete for any given scarce resource, the political perspective argues, people form coalitions (Bolman & Deal, 2008). Individuals or groups with shared interests come together to pursue their issues around that resource. The old adage that "politics makes strange bedfellows" is aptly applied here (Atinc, Darrat, Fuller, & Parker, 2010; Butcher & Clarke, 2002). For example, many state legislatures in recent years have introduced bills related to carrying guns on college and university campuses. Such measures usually draw opposition from a powerful coalition comprised, on one hand, of gun-rights activists who believe any regulation of guns violates the Second Amendment to the US Constitution and, on the other, gun-control advocates who believe such measures do not go far enough. Likewise, student government initiatives that aim to limit funding for clubs and organizations that have a religious agenda (e.g., Jewish Student Union, Youth for Christ)) tend to be opposed by a coalition of student organizations from across the religious spectrum. In the political perspective, coalitions form and dissipate as different types of resources come into play.

The second concept critical to the political perspective relates to notions of power (Fairholm, 2009; Morgan, 2006). There are many forms of power that individuals and groups exert within organizations (Aims & Silk, 2008; Vigoda-Gadot, 2007). The most obvious of these is position power, or the authority vested in a person based on her or his position within the organization. Other forms of power are often equally—if not more—influential than position power, however. On college and university campuses, for example, expertise (specialized knowledge on a given subject) is a form of power that faculty frequently rely on (Coopey & Burgoyne, 2000). Charismatic authority is another form of power. When a person has no official role in an organization but holds sway with others simply by virtue of his or her personality, that person can often influence the group. Control of technology is a rapidly growing form of power in organizations. Those who control access to hardware or who have expertise with software are increasingly essential in organizations (Bolman & Deal, 2008; Morgan, 2006) and may exert their influence to secure resources. There are many other forms of power, but this list offers an overview of some of the more common types.

The political perspective, then, is an important tool for entering student affairs professionals if they understand its nuances. To that end, we offer three observations about how diversity may play out in this framework. First, this perspective revolves around the concept of scarce resources, but individuals in organizations may value certain resources over others. For some student groups, for instance, publicity is highly valued, and coverage of their events in the limited space available in the campus newspaper is what they seek. For student affairs administrators, autonomy may be cherished. The ability to tele-commute or work flexible hours, thus enabling them to better balance work and personal life, may be more important than, say, additional leave time. There are also generational differences in terms of what resources are valued. For new student affairs practitioners, opportunities for promotion and advancement may be very important. For more experienced professionals, promotion may be far less valued than, say, recognition or financial rewards. The ability to identify what is important to people is an essential skill for aspiring administrators and one that can be honed in the practicum setting.

Second, although conflict is central to the political perspective, people view (and may choose to manage) conflict in many different ways. In some cultural groups, such as Native Americans, the interests of the collective always take precedence over individual interests, so individual differences may be suppressed to promote group success. Entry-level professionals who are unused to conflict may shy away from it. Indeed, more experienced administrators may capitalize on the naïveté of their junior partners by resolving conflict on their behalf, but not necessarily in their best interests. Conflict among some seasoned professionals is a matter of timing; resolving differences immediately is appropriate in some instances, but ignoring conflict is important in other circumstances. To fully appreciate the political perspective, it is important to grasp the many approaches to conflict resolution that organizational members may employ.

Finally, the third observation about the political perspective has to do with the notions of competition and collaboration. This framework is grounded on the premise that conflict in organizations is inexorable. Yet many student affairs practitioners are averse to conflict and avoid it whenever possible. Much of our training is geared toward working collaboratively and promoting harmony. This predisposition to collaboration makes it even more compelling that entering professionals develop an appreciation for the political frame. Those who comprehend the contributions that conflict brings to organizational development are more likely to be able to identify the scarce resources associated with conflict. That ability, in turn, may lead to them to engage in and manage conflict in productive ways. If conflict over resources is inevitable, then aspiring professionals would be well served to learn how to successfully manage such conflict.

Reflection Activity

Read each of the three scenarios below and respond to these questions about each one.

1. What is the scarce resource (or resources) relevant to the scenario?
2. What coalitions might form around the issue?
3. Which coalitions might support the issue?
4. Which coalitions might oppose the issue?
5. What strategies would each group use to build support for its position?

Scenario A: You are an intern reporting to the director of residence life. A group of students and faculty members has initiated a campus discussion about transgender students and their need for gender-neutral housing on the campus. They approach the director of residence life with a request to establish designated housing for transgender students.

Scenario B: You are an intern working with the director of the student union. The university has just approved funds to expand the union. Construction will start in two years. The director asks you to assist her in putting together a planning committee.

Scenario C: You are one of three interns working in the Office of Student Activities in the fall semester. All three interns are full-time graduate students with major academic and GA responsibilities in addition to their internship responsibilities. The Office of Student Activities sponsors major campus events, including concerts, theater productions, movies, lecture series, and other types of programming. There are events three or four times per week, each sponsored by a different student organization. The director wants an intern to advise each of the sponsoring student groups. She also wants an intern to be present at every event, and asks the three of you to generate a schedule that identifies which intern will cover each event that semester.

These scenarios represent the types of organizational issues that routinely confront student affairs professionals. Your ability to identify the scarce resource that is in play and the different interests (coalitions) that may attempt to influence the allocation of that resource may enable you to appreciate the role that conflict can play in an organization. It may also provide you with the tools to resolve issues in creative ways.

The Cultural Perspective

The second framework that we believe is useful when trying to understand the workplace is the symbolic (Bolman & Deal, 2008) or cultural (Morgan, 2006) perspective. From the symbolic perspective, events that occur within organizations are not as important as the meaning that organizational members make of those events. Many aspiring administrators recognize that the culture of an organization is important but often are unable to identify specific components that comprise that culture (Armenakis, Brown, & Mehta, 2011; Mouton, Just, & Gabrielsen, 2012). We believe there are concrete elements that practitioners can identify to help make sense of the culture in their workplace.

The first element involves myths, visions, and values (Bolman & Deal, 2008) that define an organization's reason for being. Myths tell the story of the group and serve as a foundation for organizational values. They are not, however, necessarily only associated with events long past (Agyris, 2010). Consider, for example, the issue of accountability in higher education. Just a few years ago, the term was associated with a general sense of obligation to the public to use resources effectively to achieve institutional goals. Over time, however, professionals have operationalized accountability so that concrete measures are routinely collected (e.g., gains in sense of competence among student leaders, increased sense of social responsibility following a conduct hearing). The myth of accountability has, over time, become an organizational value that, to a large degree, has been incorporated into institutional vision at many campuses.

Heroes and heroines is another element that defines culture and is rife in the higher education lore (Bolman & Deal, 2008). These are the people that nearly everyone in the organization knows about (Hallett, 2003). Ask any student who works as an ambassador for the admissions office about heroes or heroines and you will likely hear the story of the first student on campus or the beloved dean who started a campus tradition. These individuals are icons to the campus community. Their actions remind organizational members of what is valued and why they engage in the work they do (Ebadollah, 2011).

Stories and fairy tales are the third component of culture that practitioners can identify (Bolman & Deal, 2008). These are tales that are commonly told that immortalize traditions (Konecki, 2006). In higher education, there are instances where campuses seem to share the same story or tale. For example, at many institutions there is a pervasive tale that if a student's roommate commits suicide, that surviving roommate will earn all As that semester. Stories of ghosts that haunt campus buildings are rampant. Other stories relate the accidents that led to great discoveries or the injured athlete who inspired teammates to overcome insurmountable odds to win a big game. The telling and retelling of such stories bind organizational members together in a shared conceptualization of what it means to belong.

Ceremonies are, perhaps, the most recognizable element of organizational culture. These are elaborate observances that instill a sense of continuity and security (Bolman & Deal, 2008; Kondra & Hurst, 2009). Higher education is rife with ceremonies. Convocation, a major annual event on many campuses, typically involves faculty and administrators clad in full regalia, leading matriculating students in a parade across campus to some central gathering place (often a chapel at small institutions). Commencement exercises are marked by similar processionals, but at these events, graduating students also wear caps and gowns. The style of the regalia, the length of the sleeves on a gown, the color of the hoods worn by those with advanced degrees—all are dictated by tradition and cross institutional boundaries. Such ceremonies are so woven into the fabric of campus life that all one needs to do is remember that they are important elements of the institutional culture.

Rituals, on the other hand, may be less obvious and vary from unit to unit across campus (Bolman & Deal, 2008). Rituals take place more frequently and are less grand than, but equally as important as, ceremonies. These are the events that provide structure to daily life in the workplace (Stebbins & Dent, 2011). For instance, in some offices, each day starts with people chatting informally over a cup of coffee. Many departments hold weekly meetings, a ritual that offers stability to the workweek. Celebrating birthdays, decorating offices for holidays, and disseminating weekly announcements to all staff members are rituals that can be readily identified. Indeed, it is through rituals that newcomers to an organization are inculcated with the organization's traditions and gain a sense of belonging.

Finally, humor, play, and metaphor encourage risk taking and experimentation in the work setting (Bolman & Deal, 2008; Schein, 2004). Practical jokes during times of high stress can alleviate tension and allow coworkers to see matters in a new light. We know of one instance when every time the director was out of town and the associate director was left in charge, she would send a daily update to the director recapping actions she had allegedly taken that day. One day she reported she had awarded everyone in the unit a 10% raise. On another occasion, she announced the establishment of a daycare center for children of office staff—located in the director's office. In another update she explained that she had given everyone the day off in honor of National Talk Like a Parrot Day. Most important, the associate director made sure to copy all staff in these daily updates. This sort of playful humor provides shared experiences that bind coworkers together.

Collectively, these six elements illustrate events and actions that those entering the workplace can actively observe to gain an understanding of the unit's culture. Gaining such a sense is important for practicum students who may have only a limited amount of time to learn as much about an office as possible. So we encourage aspiring student affairs administrators to look for the stories, heroes and heroines, rituals, and other rudiments of culture that will assist you in facilitating your transition to the workplace.

Although the elements previously described are universal to organizational culture, it is equally essential to note that these elements play out quite uniquely in diverse contexts, and it is critical to attend to those differences (Gabriel, 2010). For purposes of this discussion, we offer four examples. To start, there are dramatic differences in campus culture by institutional type (Hirt, 2006). Working at a large research university is quite different from working at a liberal arts college, for example. At the former, student affairs administrators tend to be specialists in a single functional area (e.g., student activities, residence life). At the latter, new professionals may work in multiple areas (e.g., hall director and assistant director of student activities). At historically Black colleges and universities, there is a strong culture that staff members are surrogate family for students. At Hispanic-serving institutions, working with students' extended families is the norm. At community colleges, the culture revolves around the high touch–high volume relationship.

Clearly, these statements are gross generalizations, but we include them to make an important point. Most graduate preparation programs are housed at research universities (70%) or institutions that offer bachelor's and master's degrees (30%) (Hirt, 2006). Graduate students who hold assistantships or who engage in practicum experiences at their home institution are powerfully socialized to the norms, traditions, and values of that institutional type. The jobs they take upon graduation, however, span the spectrum of institutional types. It is essential that aspiring professionals recognize the unique attributes of culture at different institutional types. By explaining the elements that operationalize culture, we hope to provide developing administrators with the tools they need to discover the culture of their work setting.

Differences in culture by functional area are equally important to aspiring administrators. In fact, graduate students may want to consider these differences when contemplating career interests. For instance, it is well known that residential life operates 24 hours a day, 7 days a week. This requires professionals who can thrive in a culture where evening and weekend demands are the norm and may arise at any time. Other areas of student affairs also compel administrators to work outside normal business hours, but under different circumstances. Consider those who manage campus activities such as concerts, theater productions, or movie series. These events take place during evenings and weekends but are scheduled well in advance so that people have a greater degree of control over their work schedules. In still other functional areas such commitments outside of regular business hours are far less frequent (e.g., student conduct and career services). Learning about the general cultural norms of functional areas may enable those entering the profession to select an arena that best suits not only their professional interests, but their personal needs.

In most instances, cultural differences between functional areas cross institutional boundaries. That is, working in student activities at a liberal arts college may be more similar to working in student activities at a master's institution than it is to working in residential life at the same liberal arts institution. Indeed, these cross-institutional bonds have been formalized through professional associations like National Orientation Directors Association (NODA), the National Association of Campus Activities (NACA), and the Association of College and University Housing Officers-International (ACUHO-I). These groups serve to further socialize professionals to the culture of the functional area regardless of the type of institution at which they work.

It is also important to note two types of functional areas, each with its own distinctive culture. The older functional areas in student affairs administration are based on services: providing housing, activities, leadership, or career services. Those who work in functionally based units learn about all aspects of a service and provide that service to all students. Those in residence life, for instance, become familiar with the assignment process, maintenance and housekeeping duties, business operations, and other aspects of the housing function. In the past three decades, the student affairs units that have emerged have been population-based: centers for women, Black students, Latino/as, Native Americans, GLBTQ students, and veterans, to name but a few. Those working in these offices are knowledgeable about the student group they serve, and their job is to refer students to functionally based offices as appropriate. There are fundamental differences in culture between functional- versus population-based operations. The practicum experience is an opportunity for developing professionals to explore these cultural differences and learn whether they are better suited for one environment or another.

Finally, there are cultural differences that have nothing to do with institutional type, functional area, or type of service. Rather, they are based on the individuals within the work setting and differences by generation. There is a wealth of literature on Baby Boomers, Generation X, Generation Y, and the Millennials and our intention is not to repeat it here. Suffice it to say that different generations have different values that play out in the workplace. For example, Boomers typically value structure and routine. They are used to investing time and energy over a long period of time before reaping any rewards from their work. Millennials, on the other hand, seek flexibility in their work schedules and opportunities to telecommute. They are tech savvy and used to immediate feedback; their Boomer counterparts may prefer face-to-face communication and performance evaluation at regularly scheduled intervals. Generation Xers who lived through difficult economic times in the 1980s tend to be independent and individualistic. They value work–life balance and may not express interest in advancement or may move to another institution to pursue that balance; Boomers tend to be more loyal; moving to another institution is a less frequent occurrence. Again, we do not mean that all members of a generation act in the same way. Rather, we simply believe that those entering the profession need to be aware of how generational differences are enacted in the workplace. The practicum provides a unique opportunity to aspiring professionals to pay attention to these differences and to learn how to adapt to successfully interact with coworkers from all generations.

Reflection Activity

Think about your internship workplace and what you know about the institution. On a piece of paper, create a table that consists of six rows and three columns. Label the rows as follows: Myths, Visions and Values; Heroes and Heroines; Stories and Fairy Tales; Ceremonies; Rituals; and Humor, Metaphor and Play.

1. Think about each of these six elements of culture and, in Column 1, list all the examples you can think of for each element that you have observed in your internship setting or on your campus.
2. Talk to your work colleagues and ask them to explain what these symbols or examples (artifacts) mean to them and make note of their responses in Column 2.
3. In Column 3, write yourself notes about how these artifacts might be used in your own daily practice.

Conclusion

In summary, many graduate students believe that the internships they pursue as part of their degree requirements are opportunities to test their interest in a certain job. That is certainly a major component of the practicum. However, all work takes place in an organizational setting, and all organizational settings have unique characteristics. The intern who can look at workplace issues from a variety of perspectives gains a richer, more nuanced understanding of that issue and that organization. In the end, that student intern is better situated to generate multiple responses to any given issue and to succeed in a variety of organizational settings and professional capacities.

References

Agyris, C. (2010). *Organizational traps: Leadership, culture, organizational design.* Oxford, UK: Oxford University Press.

Aims, J. M., & Silk, M. L. (2008). The philosophy and politics of quality in qualitative organizational research. *Organizational Research Methods, 11,* 456–480.

Andrews, M., & Kacmar, K. M. (2001). Discriminating among organizational politics, justice, and support. *Journal of Organizational Behavior, 22,* 347–366.

Armenakis, A., Brown, S., & Mehta, A. (2011). Organizational culture: Assessment and transformation. *Journal of Change Management, 11,* 305–328.

Atinc, G., Darrat, M., Fuller, B., & Parker, W. (2010) Perceptions of organizational politics: A meta-analysis of theoretical antecedents. *Journal of Managerial Issues, 22,* 494–513.

Bergquist, W. H., & Pawlak, K. (2008). *Engaging the six cultures of the academy.* San Francisco, CA: Jossey-Bass.

Bolman, L. G., & Deal, T. E. (2008). *Reframing organizations: Artistry, choice, and leadership* (4th ed.). San Francisco, CA: Jossey-Bass.

Burns, J. Z., & Otte, F. L. (1999). Implications of leader-member exchange theory and research for human resource development research. *Human Resource Development Quarterly, 10,* 225–248.

Butcher, D., & Clarke, M. (2002). Organizational politics: The cornerstone for organizational democracy. *Organizational Dynamics, 31,* 35–46.

Coopey, J., & Burgoyne, J. (2000). Politics and organizational learning. *Journal of Management Studies, 37,* 869–886.

Dooley, K., Kevin, J., Douglas, L., & Dietz, A. S. (2013). Introduction to the special issue on nonlinear organizational dynamics. *Nonlinear Dynamics, Psychology, and Life Sciences, 17,* 1–2.

Ebadollah, A. (2011). Organizational culture and productivity. *Procedia-Social and Behavioral Sciences, 15,* 772–776.

Fairholm, G. W. (2009). *Organizational power politics: Tactics in organizational leadership.* Santa Barbara, CA: Praeger/ABC CLIO.

Ferris, G. R., & Treadway, D. C. (2012). *Politics in organizations: Theory and research considerations.* New York, NY: Routledge.

Gabriel, R. J. (2010). Tying diversity to organizational culture. *Law Library Journal, 3,* 507.

Gebauer, H., Putz, F., Fischer, T., & Fleisch, E. (2009). Service orientation of organizational structures. *Journal of Relationship Marketing, 8,* 103–126.

Guest, D. E. (2011). Human resource management: Still searching for some answers. *Human Resource Management Journal, 21,* 3–13.

Hallett, T. (2003). Symbolic power and organizational culture. *Sociological Theory, 21,* 128–149.

Harris, K., & Rosen, C. C. (2009). The emotional implications of organizational politics: A process model. *Human Relations, 62,* 27–57.

Heine, K., & Rindfleisch, H. (2013). Organizational decline: A synthesis of insights from organizational ecology, path dependence, and the resource-based view. *Journal of Organizational Change Management, 26,* 8–28.

Hirt, J. B. (2006). *Where you work matters.* Lanham, MD: University Press of America.

Jacobs, R. L., & Park, Y. (2009). A proposed conceptual framework of workplace learning: Implications for theory development and research in human resource development. *Human Resource Development Review, 8,* 133–150.

Kohlberg, L. (1969). *Handbook of Socialization Theory and Research.* New York, NY: McGraw Hill.

Kola, S. (2013). Revisiting the good and bad sides of organizational politics. *Journal of Business and Economics Research, 11,* 197–202.

Kondra, A. Z., & Hurst, D. C. (2009). Institutional processes of organizational culture. *Culture and Organization, 15,* 39–58.

Konecki, K. T. (2006). Reproduction of organizational culture: What does organizational culture recreate? *Problems and Perspectives in Management, 4*(4), 26–41.

Lawrence, J., & Ott, M. (2013). Faculty perceptions of organizational politics. *Review of Higher Education, 36,* 145–178.

Legerer, P., Pfeiffer, T., Schneider, G., & Wanger, J. (2009). Organizational structure and managerial decisions. *International Journal of the Economics of Business, 16,* 147–163.

Martinez-Leon, I. M., & Martinez-Garcia, J. A. (2011). The influence of organizational structure on organizational learning. *International Journal of Manpower, 32,* 537–566.

Morgan, G. (2006). *Images of organization.* Thousand Oaks, CA: Sage.

Mouton, N., Just, S. N., & Gabrielsen, J. (2012). Creating organizational cultures. *Journal of Organizational Change Management, 25,* 315–331.

Perry, W. G., Jr. (1970). *Forms of intellectual and ethical development in the college years: A scheme.* New York, NY: Holt, Rinehart, and Winston.

Reydon, T.A.C., & Scholz, M. (2009). Why organizational ecology is not a Darwinian research program. *Philosophy of the Social Sciences, 39,* 408–439.

Schein, E. H. (2004). *Organizational culture and leadership.* San Francisco, CA: Jossey-Bass.

Stebbins, L., & Dent, E. B. (2011). Job satisfaction and organizational culture. *Journal of Applied Management and Entrepreneurship, 16,* 28–29.

Vigoda-Gadot, E. (2007). Leadership style, organizational politics, and employees' performance. *Personnel Review, 36,* 661–683.

Walczak, S. (2005). Organizational knowledge management structure. *Learning Organization, 12,* 330–339.

Appendix 1
ACPA/NASPA Professional Competency Areas

Basic Skills Self-Assessment

To determine how to maximize the learning and experience you might garner in your supervised practice setting, it would be useful to have some information on your current and desired skills. Below are the Basic Skills that ACPA and NASPA recommend professionals have in each of the 10 competency areas they have identified.

For each of the skills listed, please:

A. Indicate your current general level of competency in the left column. Indicate in the second column the level of competency you wish to have upon receiving your degree. Use the following scale:

1 = no experience
2 = minimum level of competency
3 = moderate experience with the skill
4 = high level of competency

B. In the "This Practicum" column select the 2 skills/experiences you want to work on in each of the 10 competencies during this supervised practice.

C. For each of the 2 skills you select, identify the activities/behaviors you will engage in during your internship to help you learn/experience more about that skill.

Sample

Assume your internship is in an academic advising office for students who have not yet declared a major. Below is a partial list of the basic skills associated with Advising and Helping (See Table A1.1). In this case, you have indicated that you have a minimum level of competency with respect to Active Listening and would like to have a high level of skill in this area before you graduate. You have also indicated you have no experience pursuing Multiple Objectives with students and would like to have a high level of skill before completing your degree. So, you selected these 2 skills (Exhibit Active Listening and Pursue Multiple

Table A1.1 How to complete the ACPA/NASPA's Basic Skills Assessment

Level Now	Desired Level	Item	This Practicum	How
		Advising & Helping		
2	4	Exhibit active listening skills (e.g., appropriately establishing interpersonal contact, paraphrasing, perception checking, summarizing, question-ing, encouraging, avoiding interrupting, clarifying).	Yes	Have supervisor observe me advising 3 students in order to provide feedback on my active listening skills.
3	4	Establish rapport with students, groups, colleagues, and others.		
1	3	Facilitate reflection to make meaning from experience.		
2	4	Understand and use appropriate nonverbal communication.		
1	4	Strategically and simulta-neously pursue multiple objectives in conversations with students.	Yes	Audiotape 3 student advising sessions at start of internship and 3 near the end of internship. Ask supervisor to listen and give me feedback on any change in pursu-ing multiple objectives over the term of my internship.
2	3	Facilitate problem solving.		

Objectives) as those you want to intentionally work on during your intern-ship. To work on Active Listening, you will ask your supervisor to observe you in advising sessions and offer feedback on your active listening skills. To work on Multiple Objectives, you will audiotape yourself in advising sessions early in your tenure and at the end of your internship and ask your supervisor to review those tapes with you to see if there was any change in your performance over time.

Be sure to select 2 skills from each of the 10 competency areas found in Table A1.2. If your internship does not lend itself to one of the 10 competencies, you may select more than 2 skills from another area, as long as you end up with 20 skills you intentionally want to improve during this internship. Then be sure to write your job description or internship contract to include objectives that will allow you to enact the strategies you have identified in the How column.

Level Now	*Desired Level*	*Item*	*This Practicum*	*How*
		Advising & Helping		
		Exhibit active listening skills (e.g., appropriately establishing interpersonal contact, paraphrasing, perception checking, summarizing, questioning, encouraging, avoiding interrupting, clarifying).		
		Establish rapport with students, groups, colleagues, and others.		
		Facilitate reflection to make meaning from experience.		
		Understand and use appropriate nonverbal communication.		
		Strategically and simultaneously pursue multiple objectives in conversations with students.		
		Facilitate problem solving.		
		Facilitate individual decision making and goal setting.		
		Challenge and encourage students and colleagues effectively.		
		Know and use referral sources (e.g., other offices, outside agencies, knowledge sources), and exhibit referral skills in seeking expert assistance.		
		Identify when and with whom to implement appropriate crisis management and intervention responses.		
		Maintain an appropriate degree of confidentiality that follows applicable legal and licensing requirements, facilitates the development of trusting relationships, and recognizes when confidentiality should be broken to protect the student or others.		
		Recognize the strengths and limitations of one's own worldview on communication with others (e.g., how terminology could either liberate or constrain others with different gender identities, sexual orientations, abilities, cultural backgrounds).		
		Actively seek out opportunities to expand one's own knowledge and skills in helping students with specific concerns (e.g., suicidal students) as well as interfacing with specific populations within the college student environment (e.g., student veterans).		

(Continued)

Level Now	Desired Level	Item	This Practicum	How

Assessment, Evaluation, & Research

Differentiate among assessment, program review, evaluation, planning, and research and the methodologies appropriate to each.

Effectively articulate, interpret, and use results of AER reports and studies, including professional literature.

Facilitate appropriate data collection for system/department-wide assessment and evaluation efforts using up-to-date technology and methods.

Assess trustworthiness and other aspects of quality in qualitative studies and assess the transferability of these findings to current work settings.

Assess quantitative designs and analysis techniques, including factors that might lead to measurement problems, such as those relating to sampling, validity, and reliability.

Explain the necessity to follow institutional and divisional procedures and policies (e.g., IRB approval, informed consent) with regard to ethical assessment, evaluation, and other research activities.

Explain to students and colleagues the relationship of AER processes to learning outcomes and goals.

Identify the political and educational sensitivity of raw and partially processed data and AER results, handling them with appropriate confidentiality and deference to the organizational hierarchy.

Align program and learning outcomes with organization goals and values.

Equity, Diversity, & Inclusion

Identify the contributions of similar and diverse people within and to the institutional environment.

Integrate cultural knowledge with specific and relevant diverse issues on campus.

Assess and address one's own awareness of EDI, and articulate one's own differences and similarities with others.

Level Now	Desired Level	Item	This Practicum	How
		Demonstrate personal skills associated with EDI by participating in activities that challenge one's beliefs.		
		Facilitate dialogue effectively among disparate audiences.		
		Interact with diverse individuals and implement programs, services, and activities that reflect an understanding and appreciation of cultural and human differences.		
		Recognize the intersectionality of diverse identities possessed by an individual.		
		Recognize social systems and their influence on people of diverse backgrounds.		
		Articulate a foundational understanding of social justice and the role of higher education, the institution, the department, the unit, and the individual in furthering its goals.		
		Use appropriate technology to aid in identifying individuals with diverse backgrounds as well as assessing progress towards successful integration of these individuals into the campus environment.		
		Design culturally relevant and inclusive programs, services, policies, and practices.		
		Demonstrate fair treatment to all individuals and change aspects of the environment that do not promote fair treatment.		
		Analyze the interconnectedness of societies worldwide and how these global perspectives impact institutional learning.		

Ethical Professional Practice

Level Now	Desired Level	Item	This Practicum	How
		Articulate one's personal code of ethics for student affairs practice, which reflects the ethical statements of professional student affairs associations and their foundational ethical principles.		
		Describe the ethical statements and their foundational principles of any professional associations directly relevant to one's working context.		
		Explain how one's behavior embodies the ethical statements of the profession, particularly in relationships with students and colleagues, in the use of technology and sustainable practices, in professional settings and meetings, in global relationships, and while participating in job search processes.		

(Continued)

Level Now	Desired Level	Item	This Practicum	How
		Identify ethical issues in the course of one's job.		
		Utilize institutional and professional resources to assist with ethical issues (e.g., consultation with more experienced supervisors and/or colleagues, consultation with an association's Ethics Committee).		
		Assist students in ethical decision making and make referrals to more experienced professionals when appropriate.		
		Demonstrate an understanding of the role of beliefs and values in personal integrity and professional ethical practices.		
		Appropriately address institutional actions that are not consistent with ethical standards.		
		Demonstrate an ethical commitment to just and sustainable practices.		
		History, Philosophy, & Values		
		Describe the foundational philosophies, disciplines, and values on which the profession is built.		
		Articulate the historical contexts of institutional types and functional areas within higher education and student affairs.		
		Describe the various philosophies that define the profession.		
		Demonstrate responsible campus citizenship.		
		Demonstrate empathy and compassion for student needs.		
		Describe the roles of both faculty and student affairs educators in the academy.		
		Explain the importance of service to the academy and to student affairs professional associations.		
		Articulate the principles of professional practice.		
		Articulate the history of the inclusion and exclusion of people with a variety of identities in higher education.		
		Explain the role and responsibilities of the student affairs professional associations.		
		Explain the purpose and use of publications that incorporate the philosophy and values of the profession.		

Level Now	Desired Level	Item	This Practicum	How

Explain the public role and societal benefits of student affairs and of higher education generally.

Articulate an understanding of the ongoing nature of history and one's role in shaping it.

Model the principles of the profession and communicate the expectation of the same from colleagues and supervisees.

Explain how the values of the profession contribute to sustainable practices.

Human & Organizational Resources

Describe appropriate hiring techniques and institutional hiring policies, procedures, and processes.

Demonstrate familiarity in basic tenets of supervision and possible application of these supervision techniques.

Explain how job descriptions are designed and support overall staffing patterns in one's work setting.

Design a professional development plan in one's current professional position that assesses one's strengths and weaknesses in one's current position, and establishes action items for fostering an appropriate level of growth.

Explain the application of introductory motivational techniques with students, staff, and others.

Describe the basic premises that underlie conflict in organizational and student life and the constructs utilized for facilitating conflict resolution in these settings.

Effectively and appropriately use facilities management procedures as related to operating a facility or program in a facility.

Articulate basic accounting techniques for budgeting, monitoring, and processing expenditures.

Demonstrate effective stewardship and use of resources (i.e., financial, human, material).

Use technological resources with respect to maximizing the efficiency and effectiveness of one's work.

Describe environmentally sensitive issues and explain how one's work can incorporate elements of sustainability.

Develop and disseminate agendas for meetings.

(Continued)

Level Now	Desired Level	Item	This Practicum	How
		Communicate with others using effective verbal and nonverbal strategies appropriate to the situation in both one-on-one and small group settings.		
		Recognize how networks in organizations play a role in how work gets done.		
		Understand the role alliances play in the completion of goals and work assignments.		
		Describe campus protocols for responding to significant incidents and campus crises.		
		Explain the basic tenets of personal or organizational risk and liability as they relate to one's work.		
		Law, Policy, & Governance		
		Explain the differences between public and private higher education with respect to the legal system and what they may mean for students, faculty, and staff at both types of institutions.		
		Describe the evolving legal theories that define the student–institution relationship and how they affect professional practice.		
		Describe how national constitutions and laws influence the rights that students, faculty, and staff have on public and private college campuses.		
		Explain the concepts of risk management and liability reduction strategies.		
		Explain when to consult with one's immediate supervisor and campus legal counsel about those matters that may have legal ramifications.		
		Act in accordance with federal and state/province laws and institutional policies regarding nondiscrimination.		
		Describe how policy is developed in one's department and institution, as well as the local, state/province, and federal levels of government.		
		Identify the major policy makers who influence one's professional practice at the institutional, local, state/province, and federal levels of government.		
		Identify the internal and external special interest groups that influence policy makers at the department, institutional, local, state/province, and federal levels.		
		Describe the public debates surrounding the major policy issues in higher education, including access, affordability, accountability, and quality.		

Level Now	Desired Level	Item	This Practicum	How
		Describe the governance systems at one's institution, including the governance structures for faculty, staff, and students.		
		Describe the system used to govern or coordinate one's state/province system of higher education, including community college, for-profit, and private higher education.		
		Describe the federal and state/province role in higher education.		

Leadership

Level Now	Desired Level	Item	This Practicum	How
		Describe how one's personal values, beliefs, histories, and perspectives inform one's view of oneself as an effective leader.		
		Identify one's strengths and weaknesses as a leader and seek opportunities to develop one's leadership skills.		
		Identify various constructs of leadership and leadership styles that include but are not limited to symbolic, expert, relational, and inspirational.		
		Identify basic fundamentals of teamwork and teambuilding in one's work setting and communities of practice.		
		Describe and apply the basic principles of community building.		
		Use technology to support the leadership process (e.g., seeking feedback, sharing decisions, posting data that support decisions, using group-support website tools).		
		Understand campus cultures (e.g., academic cultures, student cultures) and collaborative relationships, applying that understanding to one's work.		
		Articulate the vision and mission of the primary work unit, the division, and the institution.		
		Explain the values and processes that lead to organizational improvement.		
		Identify institutional traditions, mores, and organizational structures (e.g., hierarchy, networks, governing groups, nature of power, policies, goals, agendas, and resource allocation processes) and how they influence others to act in the organization.		
		Explain the advantages and disadvantages of different types of decision-making processes (e.g., consensus, majority vote, and decision by authority).		

(Continued)

Level Now	Desired Level	Item	This Practicum	How
		Think critically and creatively, and imagine possibilities for solutions that do not currently exist or are not apparent.		
		Identify and then effectively consult with key stakeholders and those with diverse perspectives to make informed decisions.		
		Explain the impact of decisions on diverse groups of people, other units, and sustainable practices.		
		Articulate the logic used in making decisions to all interested parties.		
		Exhibit informed confidence in the capacity of ordinary people to pull together and take practical action to transform their communities and world.		
		Identify and introduce conversations on potential issues and developing trends into appropriate venues such as staff meetings.		
		Personal Foundations		
		Identify key elements of one's set of personal beliefs and commitments (e.g., values, morals, goals, desires, self-definitions), as well as the source of each (e.g., self, peers, family, or one or more larger communities).		
		Identify one's primary work responsibilities and, with appropriate ongoing feedback, craft a realistic, summative self-appraisal of one's strengths and limitations.		
		Describe the importance of one's professional and personal life to self, and recognize the intersection of each.		
		Articulate awareness and understanding of one's attitudes, values, beliefs, assumptions, biases, and identity as it impacts one's work with others; and take responsibility to develop personal cultural skills by participating in activities that challenge one's beliefs.		
		Recognize and articulate healthy habits for better living.		
		Articulate an understanding that wellness is a broad concept comprised of emotional, physical, social, environmental, relational, spiritual, and intellectual elements.		

Level Now	Desired Level	Item	This Practicum	How
		Identify and describe personal and professional responsibilities inherent to excellence.		
		Articulate meaningful goals for one's work.		
		Identify positive and negative impacts on psychological wellness and, as appropriate, seek assistance from available resources.		
		Recognize the importance of reflection in personal and professional development.		
		Student Learning & Development		
		Articulate theories and models that describe the development of college students and the conditions and practices that facilitate holistic development.		
		Articulate how differences of race, ethnicity, nationality, class, gender, age, sexual orientation, gender identity, disability, and religious belief can influence development during the college years.		
		Identify and define types of theories (e.g., learning, psychosocial and identity development, cognitive-structural, typological, and environmental).		
		Identify the limitations in applying existing theories and models to varying student demographic groups.		
		Articulate one's own developmental journey and identify one's own informal theories of student development and learning (also called "theories-in-use") and how they can be informed by formal theories to enhance work with students.		
		Generate ways in which various learning theories and models can inform training and teaching practice.		
		Identify and construct learning outcomes for both daily practice as well as teaching and training activities.		
		Assess teaching, learning, and training and incorporate the results into practice.		

Appendix 2
Sample Practicum Contract

The following is a sample practicum contract. Although you should think creatively when creating this document, make sure that you address each item that appears in bold.

Sample

Student Information

Jane Doe
jdoe@su.edu
00 Rose Lane, Statesville, VA 23456
(H) 123.951.0000
(W) 123.231.0000

Practicum Site Supervisor Information

Jemal Smith
jsmith@su.edu
Assistant Dean of Students
107 Brodie Hall, State University, Statesville, VA 23456
(W) 123.231.0001
(FAX) 123.456.7890

Faculty Practicum Coordinator Information

Dale Jones
djones@su.edu
Associate Professor
123 Abner Hall, State University, Statesville, VA 23456
(W) 123.231.0002
(FAX) 123.567.8901

Statement of Purpose

The purpose of this practicum is to gain a better understanding of the role and function of the Dean of Students Office in mediating student disputes by assisting in the research and development of a new conflict resolution model. This practicum will also provide an opportunity to become familiar with the various programs and positions within the Dean of Students Office at State University.

Objectives and Activities

Objective 1: To assist with the development of a peer conflict resolution model proposal.
  Activities:

  a. Research conflict resolution models of other universities and suggestions from the National Association of Mediation in Education. [20 hours]
  b. Meet regularly with the site supervisor to discuss progress. [15 hours]
  c. Consult with other Dean of Students Office staff members on model components. [5 hours]

  Skills and Competencies: These activities will hone research skills, will contribute valuable information needed to tailor this model to State University, and will provide an opportunity for collaboration with many student affairs professionals.

  Time Required: 40 Hours

Objective 2: To conceptualize the logistics of the conflict resolution model.
  Activities:

  a. Draft curriculum and training outline for staff and students. [30 hours]
  b. Determine parameters of the model (e.g., size of peer educator population, target organization for recruiting). [10 hours]
  c. Identify problem-solving strategies. [20 hours]

  Skills and Competencies: By using the research from the first objective to determine the logistics of the conflict resolution model, the link from theory to practice that is so crucial in student affairs will be made. It will be necessary to weigh available resources, human and financial, in creating the model components and in planning for the implementation of the model. Strategies for problem solving will also be learned through this objective.

  Time Required: 60 Hours

Objective 3: To gain an understanding of the roles and functions of the various positions within the Dean of Students Office and the issues that confront each professional staff member.
  Activities:

  a. Review available policy manuals and other office literature. [5 hours]
  b. Attend weekly staff meetings. [30 hours]

c.   Interview office staff on their respective roles. [5 hours]
d.   Field telephone calls from students and parents and assist in problem solving. [10 hours]

Skills and Competencies: This objective will provide insight into the problems and issues of State University students and the various protocols for handling such issues within the Dean of Students Office. This objective will provide opportunities for developing professional relationships in the student affairs field. Completion of this objective will also allow for professional development through the hands-on experience of dealing with student and parental concerns.

Time Required: 50 Hours

Total Hours: 150 Hours

Site Location: The Dean of Students Office will provide space for the practicum student in room 111 Brodie Hall.

Proposed Work Schedule: The student and supervisor have agreed that the student will be in the office on Mondays and Wednesdays from 9:00 a.m. to 12:00 p.m. and Fridays from 1:00 p.m. to 5:00 p.m. Over the course of the 15-week semester, the 150-hour contract will be satisfied. Changes in the schedule will be made as needed.

Signatures

Student Signature: _____   Date: _____

Site Supervisor: _____   Date: _____

Faculty Practicum Coordinator: _____   Date: _____

Appendix 3
Reflection Journal

Directions: Fill out a journal entry weekly. Discuss it with either your on-site or faculty supervisor. Keep these journals so that at the end of the term they will be the basis for your evaluation.

Name: _____ Date: _____

1. Describe what you experienced during the past week at your internship. (Include meetings, tasks accomplished, conversations, services you delivered, etc.) Describe the experiences as fully as possible, without bias, including relevant details.
2. What did you observe about yourself, other people, policies, written material, and the physical environment during your experience?
3. Reflections: What did your experience and observations cause you to think about? Use the following perspectives to guide your reflections.
   a. How might students perceive my experience?
   b. How might staff interpret my experience?
   c. How might my experience be seen by other elements of the community (e.g., faculty, administrators, faculty)?
   d. What do existing theories or research tell me about my experience?
   e. How do my values, experiences, and preferences affect how I interpret my experience?
4. What tentative conclusions or hypotheses can I draw from my experience, observations, and reflections?
5. What actions do I need to take or what questions do I need to ask to either strengthen or disprove my tentative conclusion?

Appendix 4
Ending the Internship Experience Questionnaire

While preparing to complete the supervised practice experience, take a few minutes to reflect on this experience and to answer the following questions.

1. Thinking back to the beginning of your internship experience, what goals did you set for yourself? Now that you are almost finished with the experience, how have you met those goals?

   Goals I set   *Ways I went about meeting each goal*

2. What were some ways the staff at your internship site helped you become integrated into your new environment? Please consider the way you were integrated into the social structure as well as how you learned about policies and procedures of the site.

3. How have staff members at your site helped you prepare for leaving the site? Please consider not only ways in which you will end relationships with students and also ways in which you will finish up work tasks, say good-bye to colleagues, and leave the location.

4. What feelings are you experiencing now that you are preparing to terminate this internship experience?

Appendix 5
Site and Supervisor Evaluation

Name of Setting: _____

On-Site Supervisor Name and Title: _____

Average hours per week spent on the job: _____.

In order to improve the supervised practice, it is necessary to obtain an evaluation of your field setting and your site supervisor. I am interested in your observations, opinions about strong and weak points, and reactions to your experience. The following questionnaire contains both closed and open questions. Please feel free to make comments as appropriate. Please circle your responses and write additional comments in the space below each item.

Table A5.1 Sample site evaluation instrument

	Strongly Disagree	Disagree	Agree	Strongly Agree	NA
1. The practicum experience helped me apply theory to practice.	1	2	3	4	na
2. I always felt welcome in the setting.	1	2	3	4	na
3. Site personnel and staff members interacted with me and related to me in a colleague-like fashion.	1	2	3	4	na
4. When I started my practicum, I received a comprehensive orientation that covered the organization's mission, goals, administrative structure, and relevant policies and procedures.	1	2	3	4	na
5. As part of my on-site orientation, I learned about the organization's relationship to other departments and to the university as a whole.	1	2	3	4	na

(Continued)

	Strongly Disagree	Disagree	Agree	Strongly Agree	NA
6. My site supervisor and I established my goals and objectives early in my practicum.	1	2	3	4	na
7. My practicum was implemented in a timely manner.	1	2	3	4	na
8. My site supervisor met with me regularly.	1	2	3	4	na
9. My site supervisor seemed knowledgeable about his or her area of responsibility.	1	2	3	4	na
10. My site supervisor seemed to be aware of pertinent professional and current issues related to the work of the setting.	1	2	3	4	na
11. My site supervisor would be a good model for me should I choose to work in this area.	1	2	3	4	na
12. My site supervisor was receptive to suggestions I made.	1	2	3	4	na
13. My site supervisor seemed genuinely interested in what I had to say.	1	2	3	4	na
14. My site supervisor seemed genuinely interested in me as a person and as a future professional.	1	2	3	4	na
15. My site supervisor helped me assess my strengths and weaknesses as a student development worker.	1	2	3	4	na
16. I feel my supervisor knows me well enough so that I could ask him or her to be a professional reference.	1	2	3	4	na
17. I felt I had the freedom to entertain viewpoints other than those of the supervisor without prejudice.	1	2	3	4	na
18. In this experience I was allowed the freedom to develop my own style in working in the site.	1	2	3	4	na
19. The environment in the site was quite open; I was given access to information to the extent I feel is professionally appropriate for a practicum student at the site.	1	2	3	4	na

	Strongly Disagree	Disagree	Agree	Strongly Agree	NA
20. I believe I have learned a great deal and have grown professionally through my experience in this practicum.	1	2	3	4	na
21. As a result of this practicum experience I am now preparing to take an entry-level position in this (or a similar) agency.	1	2	3	4	na
22. I feel this practicum needs to be modified before students participate in it again (comment on the modifications, please).	1	2	3	4	na
23. I feel this site should be highly recommended to students considering it for a practicum.	1	2	3	4	na
24. I feel this practicum site should be discontinued.	1	2	3	4	na
25. Adequate and accurate preassignment information was available (I knew what to expect).	1	2	3	4	na
26. Ample time was available for me to accomplish desired learning.	1	2	3	4	na
27. Ample preparation time to assume responsibility was available to me.	1	2	3	4	na
28. Ample opportunity to exercise my judgment and try out new ideas was available to me.	1	2	3	4	na
29. Ample opportunity to be involved in many different functions was available to me.	1	2	3	4	na
30. Ample contact with students occurred.	1	2	3	4	na
31. Professional ethics were exemplified and discussed.	1	2	3	4	na
32. Problems of discrimination were dealt with appropriately.	1	2	3	4	na
33. The experience was well structured and designed to promote learning.	1	2	3	4	na
34. I was provided ample opportunity to observe and acquire new skills.	1	2	3	4	na
35. Ample opportunity was available to help me achieve personal objectives.	1	2	3	4	na

(Continued)

Table A5.1 (Continued)

	Strongly Disagree	Disagree	Agree	Strongly Agree	NA
36. I am completely satisfied with this fieldwork experience.	1	2	3	4	na
37. This field experience has motivated and encouraged me about entering the student affairs profession.	1	2	3	4	na
38. This experience was an invaluable aid to my professional development.	1	2	3	4	na
39. I honestly gave all I could to being a great practicum student.	1	2	3	4	na
40. Please include any other comments about your student development site experience.					
41. Please include any comments about the practicum program in general.					

Name (please print)   Signature   Date

_____   _____   _____

Appendix 6
Ethical Professional Practice

The Ethical Professional Practice competency area pertains to the knowledge, skills, and attitudes needed to understand and apply ethical standards to one's work. While ethics is an integral component of all the competency areas, this competency area focuses specifically on the integration of ethics into all aspects of self and professional practice.

Basic

One should be able to:

- articulate one's personal code of ethics for student affairs practice, which reflects the ethical statements of professional student affairs associations and their foundational ethical principles;
- describe the ethical statements and their foundational principles of any professional associations directly relevant to one's working context;
- explain how one's behavior embodies the ethical statements of the profession, particularly in relationships with students and colleagues, in the use of technology and sustainable practices, in professional settings and meetings, in global relationships, and while participating in job search processes;
- identify ethical issues in the course of one's job;
- utilize institutional and professional resources to assist with ethical issues (e.g., consultation with more experienced supervisors and/or colleagues, consultation with an association's Ethics Committee);
- assist students in ethical decision making and make referrals to more experienced professionals when appropriate;
- demonstrate an understanding of the role of beliefs and values in personal integrity and professional ethical practices;
- appropriately address institutional actions that are not consistent with ethical standards; and
- demonstrate an ethical commitment to just and sustainable practices.

Intermediate

One should be able to:

- explain how one's professional practice also aligns with one's personal code of ethics and ethical statements of professional student affairs associations;
- identify and seek to resolve areas of incongruence between personal, institutional, and professional ethical standards;
- address and resolve lapses in ethical behavior among colleagues and students;
- recognize the legal influences on the ethical statements of different functional areas and professions within student affairs (e.g., medical professionals, counselors);
- identify and articulate the influence of various cultures in the interpretation of ethical standards; and
- articulate and implement a personal protocol for ethical decision making.

Advanced

One should be able to:

- engage in effective consultation and provide advice regarding ethical issues with colleagues and students;
- ensure those working in the unit or division adhere to identified ethical guidelines and appropriately resolve disparities;
- actively engage in conversation with staff about the ethical statements of professional associations; and
- actively support the ethical development of other professionals as well as developing and supporting an ethical organizational culture within the workplace.

Appendix 7

ACPA's Statement of Ethical Principles and Standards Approved by the ACPA Executive Committee in March, 2006

Preamble

ACPA—College Student Educators International is an association whose members are dedicated to enhancing the worth, dignity, potential, and uniqueness of each individual within post-secondary educational institutions and, thus, to the service of society. ACPA members are committed to contributing to the comprehensive education of students, protecting human rights, advancing knowledge of student growth and development, and promoting the effectiveness of institutional programs, services, and organizational units. As a means of supporting these commitments, members of ACPA subscribe to the following principles and standards of ethical conduct. Acceptance of membership in ACPA signifies that the member understands the provisions of this statement.

This statement is designed to address issues particularly relevant to college student affairs practice. Persons charged with duties in various functional areas of higher education are also encouraged to consult ethical standards specific to their professional responsibilities.

Use of This Statement

The principal purpose of this statement is to assist student affairs professionals (individuals who are administrators, staff, faculty, and adjunct faculty in the field of student affairs) in regulating their own behavior by sensitizing them to potential ethical problems and by providing standards useful in daily practice. Observance of ethical behavior also benefits fellow professionals and students due to the effect of modeling. Self-regulation is the most effective and preferred means of assuring ethical behavior. If, however, a professional observes conduct by a fellow professional that seems contrary to the provisions of this document, several courses of action are available. Suggestions to assist with addressing ethical concerns are included in the Appendix at the end of this document.

Ethical Foundations

No statement of ethical standards can anticipate all situations that have ethical implications. When student affairs professionals are presented with dilemmas that are not explicitly addressed herein, a number of perspectives may be used in conjunction with the four standards identified in this document to assist in making decisions and determining appropriate courses of action. These standards are: 1) Professional Responsibility and Competence; 2) Student Learning and Development; 3) Responsibility to the Institution; and 4) Responsibility to Society.

Ethical principles should guide the behaviors of professionals in everyday practice. Principles are assumed to be constant and, therefore, provide consistent guidelines for decision-making. In addition, student affairs professionals should strive to develop the virtues, or habits of behavior, that are characteristic of people in helping professions. Contextual issues must also be taken into account. Such issues include, but are not limited to, culture, temporality (issues bound by time), and phenomenology (individual perspective) and community norms. Because of the complexity of ethical conversation and dialogue, the skill of simultaneously confronting differences in perspective and respecting the rights of persons to hold different perspectives becomes essential.

Ethical Standards

Four ethical standards related to primary constituencies with whom student affairs professionals work, colleagues, students, educational institutions, and society—are specified.

1. Professional Responsibility and Competence

Student affairs professionals are responsible for promoting and facilitating student learning about students and their world, enhancing the quality and understanding of student life, advocating for student welfare and concerns, and advancing the profession and its ideals. They possess the knowledge, skills, emotional stability, and maturity to discharge responsibilities as administrators, advisors, consultants, counselors, programmers, researchers, and teachers. High levels of professional competence are expected in the performance of their duties and responsibilities. Student affairs professionals are responsible for the consequences of their actions or inaction.

As ACPA members, student affairs professionals will:

1.1 Conduct their professional activities in accordance with sound theoretical principles and adopt a personal value system congruent with the basic tenets of the profession.
1.2 Contribute to the development of the profession (e.g., recruiting students to the profession, serving professional organizations, advocating the use of ethical thinking through educational and professional development activities, improving professional practices, and conducting and reporting research).
1.3 Maintain and enhance professional effectiveness by continually improving skills and acquiring new knowledge.

1.4 Monitor their personal and professional functioning and effectiveness and seek assistance from appropriate professionals as needed.

1.5 Maintain current, accurate knowledge of all regulations related to privacy of student records and electronic transmission of records and update knowledge of privacy legislation on a regular basis.

1.6 Represent their professional credentials, competencies, and limitations accurately and correct any misrepresentations of these qualifications by others.

1.7 Establish fees for professional services after consideration of the ability of the recipient to pay. They will provide some services, including professional development activities for colleagues, for little or no remuneration.

1.8 Adhere to ethical practices in securing positions:
[a] represent education and experiences accurately; [b] respond to offers promptly; [c] interview for positions only when serious about accepting an offer; [d] accept only those positions they intend to assume; [e] advise current employer and all institutions at which applications are pending immediately when they sign a contract; [f] inform their employers before leaving a position within a reasonable amount of time as outlined by the institution and/or supervisor; and [g] commit to position upon acceptance.

1.9 Provide an honest, accurate, and respectful reference. If it is not deemed possible to provide a positive reference, contact the 'searching employee' to inform them of such. It is not appropriate to provide a positive reference to move an individual beyond a department or institution.

2. Student Learning and Development

Student development is an essential purpose of higher education. Support of this process is a major responsibility of the student affairs profession. Development is complex and includes cognitive, physical, moral, social, emotional, career, spiritual, personal, and intellectual dimensions. Professionals must be sensitive to and knowledgeable about the variety of backgrounds, cultures, experiences, abilities, personal characteristics and viewpoints evident in the student population and be able to incorporate appropriate theoretical perspectives to identify learning opportunities and to reduce barriers to development. Multicultural competence is a fundamental element of ethical practice.

As ACPA members, student affairs professionals will:

2.1 Treat students with respect as persons who possess dignity, worth, and the ability to be self-directed.

2.2 Avoid dual relationships with students where one individual serves in multiple roles that create conflicting responsibilities, role confusion, and unclear expectations (e.g., counselor/employer, supervisor/best friend, or faculty/sexual partner) that may involve incompatible roles and conflicting responsibilities.

2.3 Abstain from all forms of harassment, including but not limited to verbal and written communication, physical actions and electronic transmissions.

2.4   Abstain from sexual intimacy with clients or with students for whom they have supervisory, evaluative, or instructional responsibility.

2.5   Inform students of the conditions under which they may receive assistance.

2.6   Inform students of the nature and/or limits of confidentiality. They will share information about the students only in accordance with institutional policies and applicable laws, when given their permission, or when required to prevent personal harm to themselves or others.

2.7   Refer students to appropriate specialists before entering or continuing a helping relationship when the professional's expertise or level of comfort is exceeded. If the referral is declined, professional staff is not obliged to continue the relationship nor should they do so if there is not direct benefit to the student.

2.8   Inform students about the purpose of assessment and research; make explicit the planned use of results prior to assessment requesting participation in either.

2.9   Comply with the institutional guidelines on electronic transmission of information.

2.10   Provide appropriate contextual information to students prior to and following the use of any evaluation procedures to place results in proper perspective with other factors relevant to the assessment process (e.g., socioeconomic, gender, identity, ethnic, cultural, and gender related).

2.11   Discuss with students issues, attitudes, and behaviors that have ethical implications.

2.12   Develop multicultural knowledge, skills, competence, and use appropriate elements of these capacities in their work with students.

2.13   Faculty should inform prospective graduate students of program expectations, predominant theoretical orientations, and skills needed for successful program completion, as well as positions received by recent graduates.

2.14   Assure that required experiences involving self-disclosure are communicated to prospective graduate students. When the preparation program offers experiences that emphasize self-disclosure or other relatively intimate or personal involvement (e.g., group or individual counseling or growth groups), professionals must not have current or anticipated administrative, supervisory, or evaluative authority over participants.

2.15   Provide graduate students with a broad knowledge base consisting of theory, research, and practice.

2.16   Educate graduate students about ethical standards, responsibilities and codes of the profession. Uphold these standards within all preparation programs.

2.17   Assess all relevant competencies and interpersonal functioning of students throughout the preparation program, communicate these assessments to students, and take appropriate corrective actions including dismissal when warranted.

2.18   Assure that field supervisors are qualified to provide supervision to graduate students and are informed of their ethical responsibilities in this role.

2.19   Support professional preparation program efforts by providing assistantships, practical field placements, and consultation to students and faculty.

2.20 Gain approval of research plans involving human subjects from the institutional committee with over-sight responsibility prior to the initiation of the study. In the absence of such a committee, they will seek to create procedures to protect the rights and ensure the safety of research participants.

2.21 Conduct and report research studies accurately. Researchers will not engage in fraudulent research nor will they distort or misrepresent their data or deliberately bias their results.

2.22 Cite previous works on a topic when writing or when speaking to professional audiences.

2.23 Comply with laws and standards common in the helping professions related to citation and attribution of information accessed electronically where public domain status may be ambiguous.

2.24 Acknowledge major contributions to research projects and professional writings through joint authorships with the principal contributor listed first. They will acknowledge minor technical or professional contributions in notes or introductory statements.

2.25 Co-authorship should reflect a joint collaboration. When involvement was ancillary it is inappropriate to pressure others for joint authorship listing on publications.

2.26 Share original research data with qualified others upon request.

2.27 Communicate the results of any research judged to be of value to other professionals and not withhold results reflecting unfavorably on specific institutions, programs, services, or prevailing opinion.

2.28 Submit manuscripts for consideration to only one journal at a time. They will not seek to publish previously published or accepted-for-publication materials in other media or publications without first informing all editors and/or publishers concerned. They will make appropriate references in the text and receive permission to use copyrights.

3. Responsibility to the Institution

Institutions of higher education provide the context for student affairs practice. Institutional mission, goals, policies, organizational structure, and culture, combined with individual judgment and professional standards, define and delimit the nature and extent of practice. Student affairs professionals share responsibility with other members of the academic community for fulfilling the institutional mission. Responsibility to promote the development of students and to support the institution's policies and interests require that professionals balance competing demands.

As ACPA members, student affairs professionals will:

3.1 Contribute to their institution by supporting its mission, goals, policies, and abiding by its procedures.

3.2 Seek resolution when they and their institution encounter substantial disagreements concerning professional or personal values. Resolution may require sustained efforts to modify institutional policies and practices or result in voluntary termination of employment.

3.3　Recognize that conflicts among students, colleagues, or the institution should be resolved without diminishing respect for or appropriate obligations to any party involved.

3.4　Assure that information provided about the institution is factual and accurate.

3.5　Inform appropriate officials of conditions that may be disruptive or damaging to their institution.

3.6　Inform supervisors of conditions or practices that may restrict institutional or professional effectiveness.

3.7　Refrain from attitudes or actions that impinge on colleagues' dignity, moral code, privacy, worth, professional functioning, and/or personal growth.

3.8　Abstain from sexual intimacies with colleagues or with staff or whom they have supervisory, evaluative, or instructional responsibility.

3.9　Assure that participation by staff in planned activities that emphasize self-disclosure or other relatively intimate or personal involvement is voluntary and that the leader(s) of such activities do not have administrative, supervisory, or evaluative authority over participants.

3.10　Evaluate job performance of subordinates regularly and recommend appropriate actions to enhance professional development and improve performance.

3.11　Define job responsibilities, decision-making procedures, mutual expectations, accountability procedures, and evaluation criteria with subordinates and supervisors.

3.12　Provide fair and honest assessments and feedback for colleagues' job performance and provide opportunities for professional growth as appropriate.

3.13　Seek evaluations of their job performance and/or services they provide.

3.14　Disseminate information that accurately describes the responsibilities of position vacancies, required qualifications, and the institution.

3.15　Adhere to ethical practices when facilitating or participating in a selection process by [a] representing the department and institution honestly and accurately [b] periodically notify applicants of their status; [c] adhere to established guidelines, protocol, and standards for the selection process; and [d] provide accurate information about the resources available to applicants once employed.

3.16　Provide training to student affairs search and screening committee members.

3.17　Refrain from using their positions to seek unjustified personal gains, sexual favors, unfair advantages, or unearned goods and services not normally accorded in such positions.

3.18　Recognize their fiduciary responsibility to the institution. They will ensure that funds for which they have oversight are expended following established procedures and in ways that optimize value, are accounted for properly, and contribute to the accomplishment of the institution's mission. They also will assure equipment, facilities, personnel, and other resources are used to promote the welfare of the institution and students.

3.19 Restrict their private interests, obligations, and transactions in ways to minimize conflicts of interest or the appearance of conflicts of interest. They will identify their personal views and actions as private citizens from those expressed or undertaken as institutional representatives.

3.20 Evaluate programs, services, and organizational structure regularly and systematically to assure conformity to published standards and guidelines. Evaluations should be conducted using rigorous evaluation methods and principles, and the results should be made available to appropriate institutional personnel.

3.21 Acknowledge contributions by others to program development, program implementation, evaluations, and reports.

3.22 Maintain current knowledge about changes in technology and legislation that are significant for the range of institutional responsibilities in their professional domain (e.g., knowledge of privacy and security issues, use of the internet, and free speech/hate speech).

4. Responsibility to Society

Student affairs professionals, both as citizens and practitioners, have a responsibility to contribute to the improvement of the communities in which they live and work and to act as advocates for social justice for members of those communities. They respect individuality and individual differences. They recognize that our communities are enhanced by social and individual diversity manifested by characteristics such as age, culture, class, ethnicity, gender, ability, gender identity, race, religion, and sexual orientation. Student affairs professionals work to protect human rights and promote respect for human diversity in higher education.

As ACPA members, student affairs professionals will:

4.1 Assist students in becoming productive, ethical, and responsible citizens.

4.2 Demonstrate concern for the welfare of all students and work for constructive change on behalf of students.

4.3 Not discriminate on the basis of age, culture, ethnicity, gender, ability, gender identity, race, class, religion, or sexual orientation. They will actively work to change discriminatory practices.

4.4 Demonstrate regard for social codes and moral expectations of the communities in which they live and work. At the same time, they will be aware of situations in which concepts of social justice may conflict with local moral standards and norms and may choose to point out these conflicts in ways that respect the rights and values of all who are involved. They will recognize that violations of accepted moral and legal standards may involve their clients, students, or colleagues in damaging personal conflicts and may impugn the integrity of the profession, their own reputations, and that of the employing institution.

4.5 Report to the appropriate authority any condition that is likely to harm their clients and/or others.

Appendix A

Suggestions for Resolving Ethical Misconduct
    Use of This Statement (from page 1)

Initiate a private conversation. Because unethical conduct often is due to a lack of awareness or understanding of ethical standards as described in the preceding document, a private conversation between the target of inappropriate action(s) and the individual being inappropriate is an important initial line of action. This conference, if pursued in a spirit of collegiality and sincerity, often may resolve the ethical concern and promote future ethical conduct.

Pursue institutional resources. If a private conference does not resolve the problem institutional resources may be pursued. It is recommended individuals work with mentors, supervisors, faculty, colleagues, or peers to research campus based resources.

Request consultation from ACPA Ethics Committee. If an individual is unsure whether a particular behavior, activity, or practice falls under the provisions of this statement, the Ethics Committee may be contacted in writing. A detailed written description (omitting data identifying the person(s) involved), describing the potentially unethical behavior, activity, or practice and the circumstances surrounding the situation should be submitted to a member of the ACPA Ethics Committee. Members of the Committee will provide the individual with a summary of opinions regarding the ethical appropriateness of the conduct or practice in question, as well as some suggestions as to what action(s) could be taken. Because these opinions are based on limited information, no specific situation or action will be judged "unethical." Responses rendered by the Committee are advisory only and are not an official statement on behalf of ACPA.

    Please contact the ACPA Executive Director for more information.

Appendix B

Ethical Foundations of this Document
    The principles that provide the foundation for this document are:

Act to benefit others. Service to humanity is the basic tenet underlying student affairs practice. Hence, the student affairs profession exists to: [a] promote cognitive, social, physical, intellectual, and spiritual development of students; [b] bring an institution-wide awareness of the interconnectedness of learning and development throughout the institution in academic, service, and management functions; [c] contribute to the effective functioning of the institution; and [d] provide programs and services consistent with this principle.

Promote justice. Student affairs professionals are committed to assuring fundamental fairness for all persons within the academic community. The values of impartiality, equity, and reciprocity are basic. When there are greater needs than resources available or when the interests of constituencies conflict, justice requires honest consideration of all claims and requests and equitable (not necessarily equal) distribution of goods and services. A crucial aspect of promoting justice is demonstrating respect for human differences and opposing intolerance of these differences. Important human differences include, but are not limited to, characteristics such as ability, age, class, culture, ethnicity, gender, gender identity, race, religion, or sexual orientation.

Respect autonomy. Student affairs professionals respect and promote autonomy and privacy. This includes the rights of persons whose cultural traditions elevate the importance of the family over the importance of the individual to make choices based on the desires of their families if they wish. Students' freedom of choice and action are not restricted unless their actions significantly interfere with the welfare of others or the accomplishment of the institution's mission.

Be faithful. Student affairs professionals make all efforts to be accurate in their presentation of facts, honor agreements, and trustworthy in the performance of their duties.

Do no harm. Student affairs professionals do not engage in activities that cause either physical or psychological damage to others. In addition to their personal actions, student affairs professionals are especially vigilant to assure that the institutional policies do not:

[a] hinder students' opportunities to benefit from the learning experiences available in the environment; [b] threaten individuals' self-worth, dignity, or safety; or [c] discriminate unjustly or illegally. Student affairs professionals are expected to understand that students from non-dominant cultures and groups that differ from the majority may feel harmed by attitudes and processes that are considered harmless by members of the dominant (i.e. majority) group.

Virtues: Habitual Behavior

The virtues that student affairs educators should work to develop are based on widely accepted ideas about the characteristics of people in helping professions who are consistently ethical in their choices and behavior. Virtues differ from principles in that they are related to specific contexts and demonstrate personal characteristics that people in that context, in this case the student affairs profession, value. Virtues balance principles in that they are somewhat flexible and reflect the means by which a person acts on values. The four virtues associated with this profession are prudence, integrity, respectfulness, and benevolence.

Self-regarding virtues. Prudence and integrity are virtues related to the behavior of a person in a particular situation. Prudence signifies thoughtfulness and unwillingness to jump to conclusions. Integrity signifies consistency and wholeness; a lack of dramatic behavioral differences from one situation to another.

Other-regarding virtues. Respectfulness and benevolence are virtues that describe a person's treatment of others. Respectful persons are prudent—they take time to think about appropriate responses to others in unfamiliar situations. Respectfulness is also connected to benevolence, the consistent habit of taking other people's well-being into consideration.

Context: Finding Patterns of Meaning and Developing Ethical Perspectives

Because our campuses are comprised of people from all over the world, have official connections with institutions in many countries, and also serve people who are Americans with significant allegiance to non-dominant cultures, it is important to take context into account when addressing ethical concerns. There are three frames of reference that should be considered: culture, temporality, and phenomenology.

Culture. Every culture has its own ideas about values, virtues, social and family roles, and acceptable behavior. Cultures may be grounded in ethnicity, faith, gender, generation, sexual orientation, physical ability, or geographic area to name a few. Every campus also has a range of cultures based on work status or location as well as a dominant culture of its own. Ethical dilemmas often arise among or between people from different cultures. Ethical decision-making suggests that the values of relevant cultures be examined when dilemmas arise and overt conversations about conflicting values take place, if necessary.

Temporality. This term suggests that an awareness of time-related issues be present. These include the duration of the problem, the urgency of its resolution, the time of the academic year, the duration of the relationships among the people involved, and the "spirit of the times" or Zeitgeist.

Phenomenology. All persons have both cultural roots and individual attributes that shape their perspectives. Phenomenology refers to the personal and individual points of view of the persons involved in the situation. Both justice and prudence require that decision makers do not assume anything about a person's perspective based on cultural background until that perspective is understood in both its individual and its cultural contexts.

References for Additional Information

Fried, J. (2003). Ethical standards and principles. In S. Komives, D. Woodard, & Associates (Eds.), *Student services: A handbook for the profession* (4th ed., pp. 107–127). San Francisco: Jossey-Bass.

Kitchener, K. (1985). Ethical principles and ethical decisions in student affairs. In H. Canon & R. Brown (Eds.), *Applied ethics in student services* (New Directions in Student Services, No. 30, pp.17–30). San Francisco: Jossey-Bass.

Meara, N., Schmidt, L., & Day, J. (1996). A foundation for ethical decisions, policies and character. *The Counseling Psychologist, 24*, 4–77.

Appendix 8

CAS Statement of Shared Ethical Principles[1]

The Council for the Advancement of Standards in Higher Education (CAS) has served as a voice for quality assurance and promulgation of standards in higher education for over twenty-five years. CAS was established to promote inter-association efforts to address quality assurance, student learning, and professional integrity. It was believed that a single voice would have greater impact on the evaluation and improvement of services and programs than would many voices speaking for special interests by individual practitioners or by single-interest organizations.

CAS includes membership of over 35 active professional associations and has established standards in over 30 functional areas. It has succeeded in providing a platform through which representatives from across higher education can jointly develop and promulgate standards of good practice that are endorsed not just by those working in a particular area, but by representatives of higher education associations.

CAS often cites George Washington, who said, "Let us raise a standard to which the wise and honest can repair." CAS has raised standards; it is now time to focus on the attributes, such as wisdom and honesty, of those professionals who would use the standards.

Professionals working to provide services in higher education share more than a commitment to quality assurance and standards of practice. A review of the ethical statements of member associations demonstrates clearly that there are elements of ethical principles and values that are shared across the professions in higher education.

Most of the member associations represented in CAS are guided by ethical codes of professional practice enforced through the prescribed channels of its association. CAS acknowledges and respects the individual codes and standards of ethical conduct of their organizations. From these codes, CAS has created a statement of shared ethical principles that focuses on seven basic principles that form the foundation for CAS member association codes: autonomy, non-malfeasance, beneficence, justice, fidelity, veracity, and affiliation. This statement is not intended to replace or supplant the code of ethics of any professional association; rather, it is intended to articulate those shared ethical principles. It is our hope that by articulating those shared beliefs, CAS can promulgate a better understanding of the professions of those in service to students and higher education.

Principle I—Autonomy

We take responsibility for our actions and both support and empower an individual's and group's freedom of choice.

- We strive for quality and excellence in the work that we do
- We respect one's freedom of choice
- We believe that individuals, ourselves and others, are responsible for their own behavior and learning
- We promote positive change in individuals and in society through education
- We foster an environment where people feel empowered to make decisions
- We hold ourselves and others accountable
- We study, discuss, investigate, teach, conduct research, and publish freely within the academic community
- We engage in continuing education and professional development

Principle II—Non-Malfeasance

We pledge to do no harm.

- We collaborate with others for the good of those whom we serve
- We interact in ways that promote positive outcomes
- We create environments that are educational and supportive of the growth and development of the whole person
- We exercise role responsibilities in a manner that respects the rights and property of others without exploiting or abusing power

Principle III—Beneficence

We engage in altruistic attitudes and actions that promote goodness and contribute to the health and welfare of others.

- We treat others courteously
- We consider the thoughts and feelings of others
- We work toward positive and beneficial outcomes

Principle IV—Justice

We actively promote human dignity and endorse equality and fairness for everyone.

- We treat others with respect and fairness, preserving their dignity, honoring their differences, promoting their welfare

- We recognize diversity and embrace a cross-cultural approach in support of the worth, dignity, potential, and uniqueness of people within their social and cultural contexts
- We eliminate barriers that impede student learning and development or discriminate against full participation by all students
- We extend fundamental fairness to all persons
- We operate within the framework of laws and policies
- We respect the rights of individuals and groups to express their opinions
- We assess students in a valid, open, and fair manner and one consistent with learning objectives
- We examine the influence of power on the experience of diversity to reduce marginalization and foster community

Principle V—Fidelity

We are faithful to an obligation, trust, or duty.

- We maintain confidentiality of interactions, student records, and information related to legal and private matters
- We avoid conflicts of interest or the appearance thereof
- We honor commitments made within the guidelines of established policies and procedures
- We demonstrate loyalty and commitment to institutions that employ us
- We exercise good stewardship of resources

Principle VI—Veracity

We seek and convey the truth in our words and actions.

- We act with integrity and honesty in all endeavors and interactions
- We relay information accurately
- We communicate all relevant facts and information while respecting privacy and confidentiality

Principle VII—Affiliation

We actively promote connected relationships among all people and foster community.

- We create environments that promote connectivity
- We promote authenticity, mutual empathy, and engagement within human interactions

When professionals act in accordance with ethical principles, program quality and excellence are enhanced and ultimately students are better served. As professionals providing services in higher education, we are committed to upholding these shared ethical principles, for the benefit of our students, our professions, and higher education.

Some concepts for this code were taken from: Kitchner, K. 1985). Ethical principles and ethical decisions in student affairs. In H. Canon & R. Brown (Eds.), *Applied Ethics in Student services* (New Directions in Student Services, No. 30, pp. 17–30). San Francisco: Jossey-Bass.

Note

1. From *CAS Professional Standards for Higher Education* (8th ed.). Copyright © 2012 Council for the Advancement of Standards in Higher Education. Reprinted with permission. No part of the CAS Standards and Guidelines may be reproduced or copied in any form, by any means, without written permission of the Council for the Advancement of Standards.

Index

Lightning Source UK Ltd.
Milton Keynes UK
UKHW020415301020
372484UK00007B/100